The Common Sense Guide to Fixing the U.S. Government

Written by

Dan Craddock

Chapters

DISCLAIMERS

At the time of writing, the author does not hold any governmental office nor has he ever held a governmental position. The author is not a member of any political party and has a history of voting for both Democrats and Republicans. The advice and suggestions provided are based on sound common sense principles.

The author is NOT an Attorney. The material in this book is for informational purposes only and not for the purpose of providing legal advice. The opinions of the author may not reflect the opinions of an attorney and should not be construed as legal advice.

Copyright Notice

ACKNOWLEDGEMENTS

This book is a culmination of over two and a half years work in addition to years of domestic and international experience with individuals of various backgrounds, education, status, faith, ethnicity and culture.

I would like to dedicate this book to my wife Linda who has encouraged me to be creative and take risks; to my daughter, Stephanie, who has taught me persistence and standing up for my beliefs and to my son, Jeff, for his much appreciated advice on business, government and unions. In addition, this book is dedicated to my mother who taught me so much about life, people and business, who was my mentor and business advisor and who I miss every single day. I know she is up in Heaven guiding my life and the writing of this book. Also to my Dad who taught me some hard lessons in my formative years and the value of truth and honesty.

I also want to give credit to my editor who was invaluable in the production of this book. I am so grateful for her scholarly assistance, hard work and great advice. She was a Godsend at my time of need and continues to be someone I look up to and admire.

In addition, I must thank all my friends and family who directly or indirectly influenced the writing of this book.

CHAPTER 1

INTRODUCTION

"Government, even in its best state, is but a necessary evil; in its worst state, an intolerable one."
- Thomas Paine[1]

Definition of Common Sense by Merriam-Webster: *sound and prudent judgment based on a simple perception of the situation or facts[2]*

You might have heard the adage that common sense is not so common any more. Well, it's truer today than it has ever been. Things used to be black and white, straightforward and based on truth, morals, ethics and personal accountability. Today society is a major influencer of how we think and what our priorities are. Political correctness is in vogue and individual accountability has been placed on the back burner and replaced with the collective.

The number one issue in America and the number one reason why this country is in trouble is the lack of private sector jobs. By following the simple steps in this book, unemployment can be reduced significantly and bring the 2.4 million Americans that have quit looking for jobs back into the labor force.[3] In addition, the United States can reduce its national debt as well as streamline the Federal Government resulting in a more responsive, responsible, and effective Federal Government.

As of December 2013, the jobless rate was 6.7% which is down from 7.0%.[4] Is this great news? Not really when you consider all the factors. There are actually six classifications of labor underutilization starting with the smallest percentage, U-1, continuing in severity and numbers to the U-6. The number that is publicized is the U-3 rate which is defined as 'Total unemployed, as a percent of the civilian labor force (official unemployment rate)'.[5] This number is down from the rate of 7.9% in December 2012 which is definitely a positive sign.

The U-6 rate is defined as 'Total unemployed, plus all persons marginally attached to the labor force, plus total employed part time for economic reasons, as a percent of the civilian labor force plus all persons marginally attached to the labor force'.[6] That's a mouthful. To clarify a little bit, the persons marginally attached to the labor force are those who currently are neither working nor looking for work but indicate that they want and are available for a job and have looked for work sometime in the past twelve months. Having said all this, the rate for the U-6 in December 2013 is 13.0% which is down from 14.4% in December 2012 but still extremely high[7].

Common sense dictates that the U-6 is the real unemployment rate and I would venture to say that the large number of people that fall into this U-6 category would agree. Just because workers have become discouraged and fallen off of the active job seekers list does not mean they should be chopped from the unemployment numbers.

Let's look at this from another angle. What would happen if we started to have a job boom? Would the U-3 rate go down? Probably not and here is my reasoning. If there was a job boom, those not included in the U-3 rate would either actively seek employment or would abandon part time work in search of full time employment. If this happened, even though the number of jobs increased, the active labor force would increase by a greater number resulting in no change or an increase in the U-3 unemployment rate. The only true number is the U-6 which is the only way to tell whether we are really adding jobs as opposed to losing part of the workforce.

Since the lack of private sector jobs is our number one issue, growing the number of private sector jobs will increase the Gross Domestic Products (GDP) and increase government revenue both state and federal. It just makes common sense to focus on getting America back on its feet and prosperous again. After the job problem in America is fixed and the economy is growing, then work can begin on issues like the environment, climate change, and alternative energy sources.

What the government is doing now reminds me of the housing crisis. When housing prices were at the top, banks were making risky loans to virtually anyone that applied and now that housing prices have bottomed out in 2012[8] and risk is low, the banks are adhering to very strict lending policies. This was the exact opposite of what should have happened in the mortgage industry. Now that the United States economy is struggling and the unemployment rate is so high, the government wants to take more of the US citizens' hard earned money, institute stricter regulations, and promote higher energy prices for the consumer.

Common sense dictates that the United States must get the economy growing, put people back to work, lower the cost of energy, and lower the tax burden to hard working Americans before the other issues plaguing Americans can be tackled. The American economy is vulnerable and in order to handle the multitude of complex issues with which it is confronted, we need a robust, growing economy, affordable energy, and a stable tax system that promotes long term job growth. The rationale behind this is simple. While moving to alternative fuels will add jobs to that sector, energy prices overall will rise and employment in the energy sector will suffer which will have an adverse effect on the economy. Adding regulations to curtail carbon emissions will increase the cost of products thus having an adverse effect on the overall U.S. economy.[9]

According to the USA Today, the risk of experiencing economic insecurity in your lifetime is 79% by the time you reach 60 years old.[10] This is incredible in a country that has such a rich history of prosperity.

This book may not be politically correct but it is common sense no matter which side of the political fence you may be standing. Together the American people can solve the economic problems but it will require working together and making important compromises. Forget being a republican or democrat. That does not matter anymore. The only thing that matters is what is best for the long term stability of this great country.

Using a little ole common sense is what is needed to fix the federal government pure and simple. There is no use for ideology and political correctness when the economy is so bad. Politicians have lost their way and are endlessly campaigning for re-election instead of concentrating on the job they were elected to do. Budget deficits, record debt, high unemployment and unsustainable entitlement programs are just some of the problems facing the nation today. In addition, as the population of the United States ages, we, as a society, become more dependent on government programs. Now that universal healthcare has been added, our dependency has increased dramatically.[11]

Capitalism now seems to be a bad word according to the Occupy Movement and is being taught in some schools as evil, a system to be weary of and a system that only helps the rich get richer.[12] This makes no sense since capitalism promotes the entrepreneurial spirit and has produced more millionaires from paupers than any other country.[13] Where else can an immigrant start their own business and become a millionaire? The sky's the limit. In a survey done by Fidelity Investments, 86% of the millionaires surveyed were self-made.[14]

Capitalism and the ideals that our founding fathers laid out in the Constitution of the United States have made this country the most desirable place to live and work on this planet. I have firsthand experience since I have worked and/or lived in communist countries as well as Muslim controlled countries. I've seen real corruption, I've seen real poverty and I've seen people really suffering to just survive. I've also seen the entrepreneurial spirit in many, many people who had no real outlet to succeed. If these people had the opportunities that the US affords to all of its citizens, they would have been great successes.

Americans take our freedoms for granted which is probably one reason why so many immigrants who come to America succeed. They embrace the US freedoms and see no limits to their success. If American citizens all followed the immigrant's lead, this nation would be a better place.

It is a loss of morals and ethics and the elusive search for ultimate power that has given capitalism a bad name. Money is not the root of all evil, the absolute love of money and power is. In every walk of life there are those who choose to walk on the wild side, to take advantage of the situation, to overstep their boundaries and let greed and power control their existence. This type of individual will never be eradicated. However, what can be done is to instill the right values, proper ethics and a sense of morality in the workplace, in the home, and in the social environment.

Why is there a move away from Christianity, ethics, and morals that have served this country so well over its short history? Why is Christianity feared by Atheists? Christianity preaches personal responsibility and charity. It promotes self-worth and the value of human life. Why could this ever be wrong? Even though the specific teachings are different, how can atheists denounce something that teaches tolerance and peace towards all men?

Granted, there are zealots in all facets of life including religion but this is not the norm.

Whether you believe in Christianity or not, how can preaching self-worth and personal responsibility be a bad thing? I respect those who believe and those who do not believe. Everyone has the right to his or her own beliefs but I have one caveat. One person's beliefs should not infringe upon another's beliefs. I've seen billboards with Atheist sayings and those with Christian sayings. If I like the message I will internalize it, if not then I will not. It is as simple as that. We can all live together and prosper.

The qualities of personal responsibility and self-worth have been replaced by political correctness and dependency. How did we get from "I am responsible for my life and my actions" to "what's in it for me?"

This book is written as a guide to inform and inspire as well as to convey the common sense approach to getting the U.S. out of these doldrums. Hopefully, this book will motivate thinking of other approaches to our common problems; to get involved, and to open up a dialogue with friends, colleagues, and your government representatives. If Americans can get past the "I'm a republican" and "I'm a democrat" and on to "I'm going to do what is best for this country regardless of party politics," then issues can be solved and America can get back on track towards prosperity. As Americans, our country is too great for us to stand on the sidelines.

Thomas Paine understood the value of having an open mind when he said: *"I have always strenuously supported the right of every man to his own opinion, however different that opinion might be to mine. He who denies to another this right, makes a slave of himself to his present opinion, because he precludes himself the right of changing it."*[15] When reading this book, I urge you to forget your political affiliation, your background, your social status, your biases, and approach this book with an open, unprotected, unfettered mind.

Personal attacks and spin do not help to meet the challenges that America faces today. Truth is what we need. There are individuals on both the left and the right who will say anything including half-truths or outright lies in order to get an agenda passed. This does not reflect the views of the average American. Truth and reality must be the order of the day. Don't get caught up in the hype, do the homework, get informed. I fell into this trap because I wanted the information to be true. I sent out an article without first doing my due diligence and later was called out because the information was false. I learned my lesson the hard way. Why is it that we have truth in advertising but not truth in politics?

I was speaking with a gentleman at the gym who was telling me he was fed up with the politics and the direction of our country. I concurred. I thought I couldn't make a difference being just one person. What I discovered was if everyone hid their heads in the sand, then apathy would result, creating an apathetic or pathetic country with outcomes we are obligated to accept. In the words of Plato *"The price of apathy is to be ruled by evil men"*.[16]

You do have a voice. You can be heard whether it is by writing emails to your Congressman, discussing the issues with your friends or family, attending town hall meetings, participating in online forums, working on a campaign or a combination of the above. Even though you think your influence is small, word of mouth can travel long distances and can affect many, many minds. Americans do not give up.

Each chapter of this book outlines one or more problems facing the U.S. I have endeavored to present the problems in sufficient detail along with many possible solutions. However, these solutions are not all encompassing. Hopefully, this book will spark other solutions and possibilities to help America regain its greatness.

CHAPTER 2

THE FED

"It is well that the people of the nation do not understand our banking and monetary system, for if they did, I believe there would be a revolution before tomorrow morning." **- Henry Ford**[17]

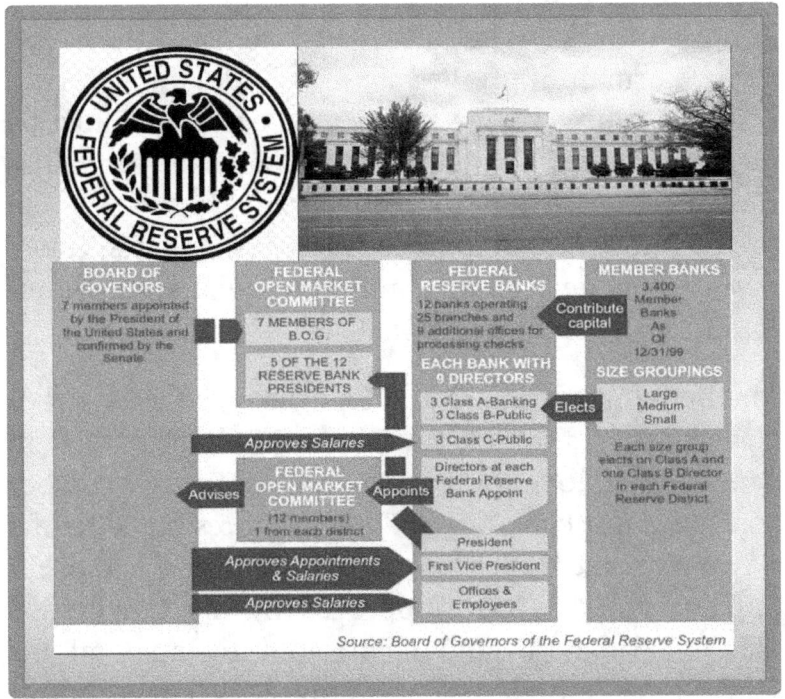

Beginning the discussion with the United States Federal Reserve System (the Fed) makes common sense. The Fed is in charge of storing and distributing money, both coin and paper currency, created by the U.S. Treasury's Bureau of the Mint and Bureau of Engraving and Printing.[18] The Federal Reserve System is a very complex and mysterious organization that is virtually a black box as far as the average American is concerned.

Some people say the Federal Reserve Chairman is the second most powerful person in the country due to the amount of control he or she has on the economy.[19] Ben Bernanke, who was the outgoing Chairman of the Fed and the primary spokesperson, was the only real glimpse Americans get into the workings of the Fed.[20] The Chairman of the Fed is a very influential person who has enormous power over the economy. Just by uttering certain words, the Fed Chairman can cause the stock market to rise dramatically or fall precipitously.[21] Common sense says this is too much power over the economy and could be misused either intentionally or unintentionally.[22]

Mr. Bernanke's term as the Chairman of the Board of Governors of the Federal Reserve System ended on January 31, 2014 and his term as a Board member continues until January 31, 2020.[23] President Obama has nominated Janet Yellen as his successor and her appointment has been approved by the Congress.[24] Her job will be a monumental one to taper off the Fed's asset purchase programs which are better known as quantitative easing (QE) which will be discussed later.[25]

The Fed is independent from the government which is a bit difficult to grasp but how it works will be explained later in this chapter. Even though the Fed is not technically a part of the federal government, it is ultimately accountable to Congress. Congress has the power to amend the Federal Reserve Act which gives the Fed its authority.[26] That being said, Congress has no control or power over what actions the Fed takes. If the Fed is not part of the government then why is it included in this book? It is a part of this book because the Fed's policies affect every American's life starting with interest rates you pay, everything you buy, and all of your investments. Furthermore, Congress has the power to limit the Fed's activities but has been hesitant or reluctant to do so.

A Brief History

The Federal Reserve System commonly referred to as the Fed, was established in December 1913 by President Woodrow Wilson when he signed the Federal Reserve Act into law.[27] Before the establishment of the Federal Reserve, there were close to 30,000 banks in the U.S. and banks were failing at an alarming rate.[28] In addition, there were huge swings in the economy and absolutely no faith and trust in the U.S. banking system.[29] The U.S. government had no choice but to come up with a way to stabilize the banking system, provide liquidity to the monetary system and regulate the banking industry.

The Fed became the United States *decentralized* Central Bank.[30] This is a misnomer. It is decentralized in the sense that it is controlled by two different entities: The Board of Governors representing the government and twelve regional reserve banks representing the private sector.[31] By having representation by both the government and the private sector, the Fed is operated as a non-partisan entity with no government control over its day-to-day activities other than the regulatory laws passed by Congress.

In 1933, Congress passed the Banking Act of 1933 better known as the Glass-Steagall Act, which called for a separation of commercial and investment banking, required government securities to be used as collateral for Federal Reserve Notes, and established the Federal Deposit Insurance Corporation (FDIC).[32] The establishment of the FDIC which insures U.S. bank deposits is the most easily recognizable portion of the Act and the one with which Americans are most familiar. The Glass-Seagall Act was subsequently repealed through the establishment of the Gramm-Leach-Bliley Act in 1999 which eliminated the restrictions against affiliations between commercial and investment banks.[33] Was this a case where overzealous regulations to a crisis caused additional problems? The U.S. banking system continued to evolve with the passing of the Banking Act of 1935, The Monetary Control Act of 1980 and, as previously mentioned, the Gramm-Leach-Bliley Act of 1999.[34] After the financial crisis of 2007-2008, Congress passed the Dodd-Frank Wall Street Reform and Consumer Protection Act of 2010 which expanded the Fed's authority to include financial stability as well as establish the Consumer Financial Protection Bureau.[35]

The U.S. has laws on the books prohibiting monopolies. If the Federal Trade Commission (FTC) and the U.S. Department of Justice (DOJ) Antitrust Division were more diligent, the banking crisis of 2008 might have been avoided. The government was not solely responsible for the crisis as weak management on the part of the banks and questionable lending practices also played a significant role in the banking crisis.[36] Common sense says that *too big to fail* should be considered a monopoly and dealt with accordingly. Being *too big* is not, in itself, a bad thing, but the potential for abuse leading to disastrous consequences with far-reaching economic effects is too great to allow.

Why do we need The Fed?

As aforementioned, there was a lack of faith and trust in the banking system (a little déjà vu?) and the economy was unpredictable.[37] In addition, there was a lack of overall central control and stability. The independent banks often lacked sufficient funds to honor withdrawals from its customers.

The Fed's original goal was to organize, stabilize, and standardize the United States monetary system.[38] It was also needed to add liquidity to the market so banks had ready cash for its customers. In addition, the Fed needed to create a currency that was elastic. In other words, control the huge swings in the economy and control inflation by making sure the prices of goods and services did not rise too quickly. The Fed also needed a means to increase or decrease the amount of money in circulation to avoid inflation or recession.[39]

Some have been critical of the Fed's regulatory performance leading up to the 2007-2008 financial crises.[40] Common sense dictates that a regulatory agency should have been able to predict, if not prevent, the financial crisis from happening. The question that has never been asked: Why was the Fed unaware a crisis was coming? As a result of the financial crisis, the regulatory responsibilities of the Fed expanded with the signing of the Dodd-Frank legislation.[41] Will this expansion of responsibilities prevent another financial crisis or will the legislation only add red tape and increase costs?

In order for the Fed to effectively control monetary policy, they must have a set of proprietary tools. In fact the Fed has three primary tools to control monetary policy:

- reserve requirements
- the discount rate, and
- Open Market Operations.[42]

The average person might not think much of these tools but they are extremely powerful and have far-reaching effects. As a matter of fact, the Open Market Operations tool is so powerful; it can cause irreparable damage to the economy if used incorrectly.

I will explain each of these tools starting with the reserve requirements. According to the Federal Reserve, "Reserve requirements are the amount of funds that a depository institution must hold in reserve against specified deposit liabilities."[43] In other words, the amount of money the depository institutions must keep in the form of cash in their vault or deposits with Federal Reserve banks.

The next tool is the Federal discount rate. This is the interest rate the Fed charges commercial banks and other depository institutions to borrow money from their regional Federal Reserve Banks.[44] Depending on the institution's general financial condition, the Fed has an interest rate structure called discount windows that fall into three categories.[45] The three categories refer to the interest rate charged to commercial banks and other financial institutions. In other words, the stronger the banks financial condition, the lower the interest rate the bank will be charged by the Fed.

The third and most important tool is the Open Market Operations (OMO) tool. As this tool is so important, the Fed created the Federal Open Market Committee (FOMC) which is responsible for setting monetary policy. The FOMC is made up of 12 people as follows:[46]

- seven members from the Board of Governors, and
- five members who are presidents of the 12 Federal Reserve Banks.

The Federal Open Market Committee (FOMC) manages open market operations (OMO) which monitor credit and the growth of the money supply as well as impact money market conditions.[47] Since the Fed already lowered the Fed discount rate to virtually zero, they no longer have this tool to control inflation, raise employment and control the money supply. What other device can the Fed utilize to keep our economy from collapsing? The answer, as was alluded to earlier, is quantitative easing or QE.[48]

Quantitative easing is a mechanism utilized by central banks to increase the money supply by purchasing government and corporate bonds from banks and other financial institutions.[49] Unlike other central banks, the Fed can only purchase U.S. Treasury and other government agency securities.[50] QE is a tool used as a last resort and employed when the Fed has utilized all other tools to stabilize the economy.

Since quantitative easing has begun, the Fed has gone through three iterations and the Fed now has almost $4 trillion in assets on its books.[51] During the third iteration of quantitative easing, the Fed has been purchasing approximately $85 billion worth of bonds every month.[52] Quantitative easing is utilized to keep interest rates low and stimulate the economy. It has definitely kept interest rates down. As to stimulating the economy, the Gross Domestic Product (GDP), which is a measure of the output of goods and services, in the third quarter of 2013 rose at an annual rate of 3.6% which is an improvement over the previous quarter.[53] Would this growth have occurred without quantitative easing? Growth comes from innovation and it appears that innovation has slowed over the years.[54] Companies have been doing more with less and cutting costs where feasible. Spending as well as demand for new technology has slowed.

Until the primary focus of businesses moves from cost-cutting back to innovation, U.S. economic growth will continue to suffer. There are currently too many distractions (i.e. Obamacare, a highly complex tax structure, political unrest, growing national debt, and increased regulations) for companies to focus on innovation. The answer is for the U.S. government to work together with business to create a consistent, cohesive business environment that facilitates long-term growth.

While interest rates have remained low and the GDP has increased, unemployment, while trending down, is 6.7% as of December 2013 which is still high.[55] The labor participation rate which has traditionally been around 66% has declined steadily since 2008 to 62.8%.[56] According to the Organization for Economic Co-Operation and Development, the labor participation rate is defined as the employment-to-population ratio.[57] This means that more people have left the workforce because they either retired or have stopped looking for work. While a modest decline can be expected with the baby boomers retiring, it appears as if more people have stopped looking for work especially the younger generation.[58]

Every action has consequences. By keeping interest rates artificially low, the Fed's actions have caused the stock market to increase to its highest levels in 2013.[59] While this is a good thing in the short-term especially for those individuals with money in the stock market, what will the effects be when quantitative easing is halted? Common sense says the Fed cannot keep buying U.S. treasury bonds every month without consequences. To stop quantitative easing when the economy is still weak may result in a double dip recession.[60] On the other hand, to stop quantitative easing when the economy is strong may cause inflation which will adversely affect the lives of every American as well as increase the government's debt interest payments.[61] Common sense dictates that the Fed should taper off slowly to cause the least harm to the economy. In a news conference on December 18, 2013, then Fed Chairman, Ben Bernanke, announced the Fed was, in fact, tapering asset purchases by $10 billion a month beginning in January 2014.[62] Since tapering started, the Dow Jones Industrial average has dropped over 7%.[63] I suspect the Fed will continue on this path for several months, analyze the economic effects and react accordingly. The Fed tends to work slowly and methodically.

Prior to 2008, the Fed was not allowed to pay interest to banks for depositing funds with the Fed. This changed with the 2008 Emergency Economic Stabilization Act more commonly referred to as the financial bailout.[64] Since banks had so many non-performing assets and were weary of lending more money, they needed an outlet where they could earn a return without adding more risk to their portfolio.

Since the financial crisis, banks have been increasing the amount of money held at the Fed to a whopping $1 trillion.[65] Before the financial crisis, banks rarely deposited over $25 billion with the Fed.[66] This extra cash should have been used to boost the economy in the form of mortgage and small business loans. However, since banks get risk-free interest from the Fed, apparently they would rather store money at the Fed than increase lending.[67] Another reason banks have not increased lending is because of the prospect of increased inflation and higher interest rates. Banks do not want to get locked into long-term commitments at today's low interest rates knowing that higher interest rates and the ability to make more money are just over the horizon.[68] Common sense dictates that the Fed should stop paying interest to banks so the banks will increase lending and therefore boost the economy.

Since the Fed is such a secret organization, common sense dictates that an organization with this much power should be more transparent. The Fed is subjected to several different audits throughout the year including audits by the Government Accountability Office (GAO), financial statement external audits, and Reserve Bank financial statement audits.[69] However, not all of the Fed's activities are subjected to these audits and herein lays the problem. What is the Fed doing behind the scenes that is not included in the current audit scheme?

SUGGESTIONS:

1. Congress needs to provide better oversight of the Fed's activities.
2. Congress needs to review and possibly amend the Dodd-Frank provisions concerning *too big to fail* and consider breaking up the large banks.
3. The Fed should continue to taper off their monthly asset buying process.
4. The Fed should stop paying interest to banks for depositing money with the Fed.
5. Congress should establish a process to increase the transparency of the Fed by allowing a full audit of its activities.

CHAPTER 3

EDUCATION

"Education is the most powerful weapon which you can use to change the world."
— Nelson Mandela[70]

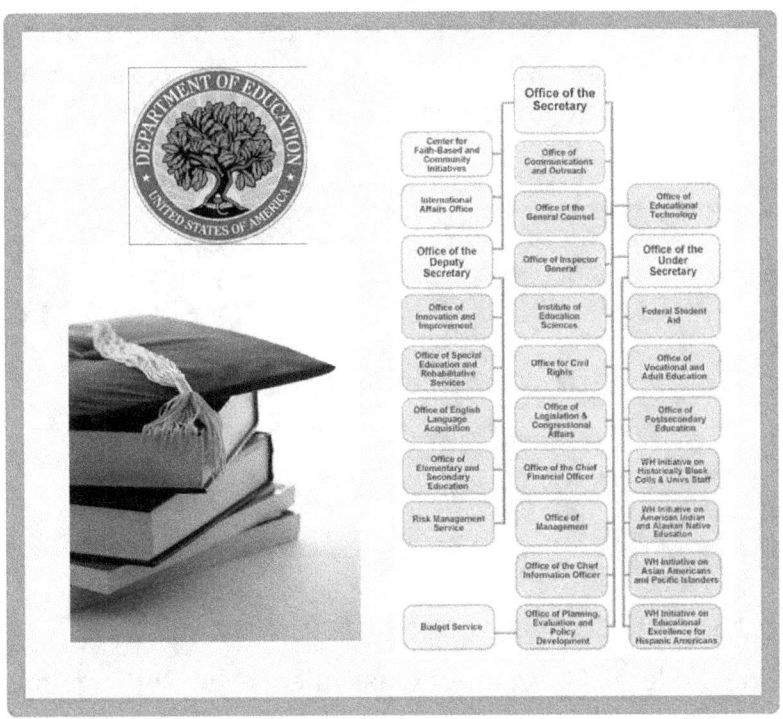

The 2012 federal budget for education and educational programs was 77.4 billion dollars[71]. While the 2013 federal budget for education was 69.8 billion dollars, this is still over 50% more than the 2009 budget of 45.4 billion dollars[72].

Year after year more and more money is thrown into our education system and our results keep getting worse and worse[73]. In my opinion, every administrations answer to this problem has been to simply throw more money at the problem and hope things will get better. Common sense says that the U.S. government needs to stop irrational spending and take a step back and analyze the problem. Administration after administration doing the same thing over and over again has not proven to be the answer.

Our Children only get one chance at a quality education. Don't they deserve the Best?

The Federal Government has filed a lawsuit against the state of Louisiana to block the 2014-2015 school voucher program that offers thousands of minority students the opportunity to attend better schools[74]. In speaking about the lawsuit, Louisiana's Governor Bobby Jindal said: "This is shameful. President Obama and Attorney General Holder are trying to keep kids trapped in failing public schools against the wishes of their parents."[75] Mr. Jindal continued with: "Make no mistake – this motion is a threat to the children in our state who only get one chance to grow up and deserve the opportunity to get the best education so they can pursue their dreams."[76] Is it appropriate for the Federal Government to sue a state for exercising their right to provide educational choices to the children of that state? Shouldn't the focus be on providing the best educational opportunities for the children no matter whether it is in a public or private school? Does the teachers union have the best interest of the student as their focus or the best interest of the teacher? Does the quality of a student's education trump teacher tenure?

If the Teachers Union has the education of the students as their primary focus, then they should embrace Charter schools and the remarkable results that have been attained in many states.[77] As a matter of fact, wherever superior results are being attained, the Teachers Union should be taking an active role in studying and analyzing those methods with the objective of duplicating or exceeding those results in the public school system instead of worrying about teacher tenure.

Education is the primary responsibility of the individual states not the federal government. It just makes common sense the closer you are to the source of a problem, the better chance you have of solving the problem. This I learned in my many years of managing Information Technology projects all over the world. The states need to take back the responsibility for educating the youth of America and quit abdicating their responsibility to the federal government.

Ever since Congress created the U.S. Department of Education in 1979, the results have progressively gotten worse while the budget continued to rise[78]. The states have willfully relinquished their responsibilities to the federal government solely because the federal government has the ability to print money. This needs to stop if the US is serious about solving the problem.

It seems like every administration, with good intention, initiates executive orders to amend or add provisions to the Department of Education. They do this because they care about specific education initiatives, it is the right political thing to do, or they have succumbed to one or more lobbyist groups. Since Congress established the Department of Education as a Cabinet level agency in 1980, I have not come across any administration reducing, eliminating or consolidating departments or programs. President Nixon in a special message to Congress in 1970 proposed that Congress create the National Institute of Education.[79] Nixon stressed local control of education but his actions created more federal bureaucracy. Wouldn't it just make common sense to analyze and streamline the organization to ensure that it is functioning in an efficient, effective and productive manner?

According to the overview of The Department of Education 2010, the Department of Education does not:[80]

- Establish schools and colleges
- Develop curricula
- Set requirements for enrollment and graduation
- Determine state education standards
- Develop or implement testing to measure whether states are meeting their education standards

Given that the US Department of Education is not tasked with doing any of the above functions, how much influence does the US Department of Education have on education in our schools? The answer is a lot more than you think. The reason why the US Department of Education has so much influence in the education of American youth is because of the federal dollars.

As long as the federal government is doling out money to the states for educational purposes, the federal government can and does place stipulations on the money.[81] For example, if the US Department of Education wants to institute certain education programs, money will be allocated based on the implementation of these programs. Since the states are in charge of developing the curricula; and we know that the closer to the problem you are, the better you are able to solve it, is the federal government helping or just adding to the problem?

There are over 4,400 employees in the Department of Education that fall under the following three offices:[82]

- Office of the Secretary
- Office of the Deputy Secretary
- Office of the Under Secretary

Under each of these offices are from five to thirteen offices performing various functions from the Office for Civil Rights to the Office of Innovation and Improvement to the Office of Career, Technical and Adult Education.[83] The overhead in this organization, which is the third largest government department, is very large. The bottom line is whether this large department is having a positive effect on the education of our youth. Given what the state's educational responsibilities are, I suspect we could do away with this department and not see a marketable difference in the test scores.

In order to effectively solve the problem, the root of the problem must be analyzed and dealt with. However, many people do not want to admit to the main causes of the problem which are:

1. The breakdown of the traditional family. One in four children in the United States is being raised by a single parent.[84] In the African

American community, the number goes up to 72%.[85]

2. The unwillingness of parents to play an active role in the education of their children. Contrary to popular belief, education is a partnership between the student, the teacher, and the parents not the student, the teacher, and the government.
3. The lack of accountability on the part of the teachers.
4. The relinquishment of the state's responsibilities to the Federal Government.

Solving the education problem in America is relatively simple but it will involve several steps:

1. Reduce the Federal Department of Education to ten employees – A department head or administrator and nine employees to develop steps to coordinate and evaluate incoming results from all 50 states. Instead of having a large bureaucracy, the department should elicit the assistance of the private sector to assist where needed.
2. Use the money saved from step number one to bolster the state education programs.
3. Dole out the money to the states based on specific results attained.
4. Initiate an independent study on why the broken home problem in America has

increased and develop a short term and long term plan to turn it around.

5. Promote parental involvement in the education of American students especially in the low income areas.

6. Create a task force made up of members from states that have had success and focus on increasing the results of the states at the bottom. Most of the states have developed task forces to improve the education in their particular state. In addition, there is also the National Governors Association (NGA) Center for Best Practices which reaches across state boundaries but more can be done utilizing technology to pass on best practices.[86] This is where the US Department of Education can assist in the facilitation of best practice sharing.

7. Advocate the use of vouchers for charter schools in all states giving students the opportunity to get the best education regardless of where they live. Currently less than a third of the state's offer some form of school vouchers.[87] These school vouchers will increase competition for students which will elevate results.

8. Fire teachers who don't or can't teach! I'll say this again – fire teachers who don't or can't teach! Don't just have them spend the time in the rubber room but actually fire teachers who are not teaching our children.[88] Education is too important to leave to

incompetent, unqualified or lazy teachers. The whole system depends on this as results cannot be elevated without it.

9. Work with the National Education Association and the American Federation of Teachers to change their hiring, transfer and firing policies so that the focus is on the students and not on the teachers. By ensuring that the students come first, the teachers will be well taken care of.

10. Increase teacher salaries and institute a bonus system! Good teachers are worth it and as long as we have the ability to weed out the bad ones, we can afford to pay the good ones what they are worth. Bonuses should not be solely based on test scores but also on the overall development of the students. This is where the Department of Education can provide value to the state schools.

11. Utilize technology in the classrooms and at home to supplement and intensify the learning experience. Sal Khan, www.khanacademy.org, has developed free online learning videos to support and enhance the learning experience in a fun, entertaining way.[89] The videos start at an elementary level and extend through high school in areas like math, science, economics, computer science, humanities as well as test preparation for SAT Math, GMAT and others. Due to the success these videos have had on student results, Sal Khan is now funded by

Bill Gates and Google.[90] Every school should be using these videos as a supplement to their curricula.

12. Make learning fun for the students.

13. Be open to new techniques to engage the students. Techniques like having a teacher wear an earpiece in order to get immediate feedback from the principle or another teacher to provide questions or add emphasis to reach the students. Sometimes all it takes is someone else to provide a different perspective in the moment to dramatically change how the information is perceived and the results attained.

14. Increase the number of hours that students attend school.

15. Change the curricula for college students obtaining teaching degrees to include state of the art training tools and techniques focused on the subject of engagement – specifically how teachers can best engage their students to attain the best results.

16. Make school uniforms including shoes mandatory and provide them free of charge to the students.   This one might be a little controversial and I actually had the same reservations at first. There are two problems that will be solved by requiring school uniforms:

a. Change of attitude leading to better students – Students tend to mellow out, learn more and conform when wearing unflattering uniforms that do not show the student as being tough and cool. The uniforms let the students know why they are at school. Having seen the change in students all over the world, it is remarkable. Since this is very successful in other countries, why not ours?

b. Families will save money. Now families don't have to buy their children cool, stylish clothes to wear every day to school. Those families who can't afford to buy expensive clothes don't have to feel bad about it.

17. Have local businesses donate the material to make the school uniforms and/or use lottery money, if applicable, to purchase the material.

18. Contract with shoe manufacturers to provide American made shoes for the students.

19. Contract with a private company to assist the United States prison system to manufacture school uniforms. By putting the prison inmates to work doing something useful for American children, it not only helps our students but gives the inmates something of which to be proud.

Our children are our future and Americans not only need to be prudent in the preservation of our world but ensure the children enjoy and embrace their childhood. Happy, well-adjusted children grow up to be good stewards of our nation. How do American citizens make sure that their children have a happy childhood? That is the question everyone wants an answer to but no one has actually pursued with vigor.

The children who are not popular or do not fit into a clique, are the ones who are more susceptible to turning into less than desirable adults. These are the children who have been ignored. They may be overweight, exhibit unsociable characteristics, may not be able to afford the latest clothes or Michael Jordan shoes and generally need help to blend in socially. I have come up with an idea that may help or be a starting point.

Beginning in high school, children join organizations or clubs or play sports to fit in or to be a part of something. These clubs or sports teams boost a person's self-confidence and self-worth as well as giving them a sense of belonging. Many children do not have the opportunity, are not asked to join these groups because they don't fit in either physically or mentally, or do not think they are worthy enough. In addition, there is safety in numbers so belonging to a group will provide some peace of mind along with all the other benefits that being a part of a group provides. Being alone and retreating into technology has worked successfully for people like Bill Gates, Steve Jobs, Mark Zuckerberg, Larry Page or Sergey Brin but is generally not the best way to prepare our children for the future.

In the formative years, children who are left out are more likely to turn to gangs, smoking, drugs or subversive groups for affirmation[91]. If a club was created for the students on the cusp, then the direction of these students could be changed to make our world a better and safer place to live.

I propose a club be created that should be available in all high schools across the country just like the debate team, science club, or football team. I envision starting this club for the unpopular kids but eventually growing to include others as well because of the popularity of the club. I was struggling with what to name the club but when my wife came up with a name as we were driving to Lake Tahoe, the light came on. The name she came up with is "UTOPIA". According to Wikipedia, the definition is: "a community or society possessing highly desirable or perfect qualities."[92] Highly desirable or perfect qualities will be an aspiration of each club member. As everyone knows, perfection cannot be attained; however, the pursuit of perfection is the goal.

I've come up with a basic outline of what should be included and what activities I would expect in the club but it is in no way all inclusive or an absolute. It is merely a guideline or a starting template.

I envision the mission of the club to be:

"To provide a safe, non-judgmental atmosphere to share, discover, prepare, encourage, work with and respect others".

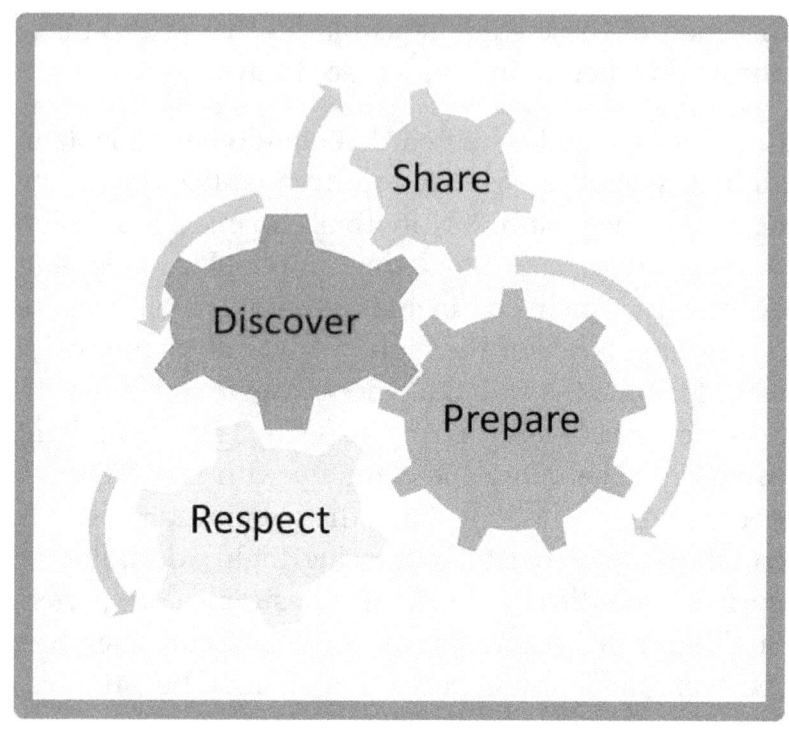

The club will focus on preparing the children for life after school. Within the club, since it will be a large organization, will be smaller pockets of students that will create a more intimate group to support and encourage each other. As a whole, the club will follow the mission to increase the involvement and socialization of the children. The smaller groups will afford greater and longer lasting individual results.

Some rules might be:

1. No bullying, harassing or verbal abuse is acceptable and grounds for removal from the group.
2. All members must actively participate in the group.
3. It is mandatory that the members learn about the others in the group. Knowing more about the group builds stronger bonds.
4. Discrimination of any kind is not allowed.
5. Actively discuss issues and keep open communication with other members of the group.
6. No subject is off limits if the discussion will serve a positive purpose.
7. Encourage other club members to exceed their expectations.

The club should have a group of central activities it is involved with as well as a charitable cause it supports. The charitable cause obviously will be different based on location and particular make-up of the club and should be chosen by the members. By collectively supporting a worthy charitable cause, the club will have a purpose and thus rally the members behind the cause.

The club activities will be focused on preparing the students not only for life in high school but for life after high school by providing real world examples of what they can realistically expect. By having real world examples of what they can expect in life by choosing a certain path will hopefully guide them towards a better path. I wish I was made privy to information like this in my formative years because it definitely would have made a positive impression.

The club activities might include:

1. Within the pocket groups, each member will interview another member and then report back to the group on the person they interviewed. The interviewer should discover the person's likes, dislikes, goals, and ambitions. In addition to establishing a commonality of purpose, the more a member knows about the other members of the group, the stronger the bonds are built.

2. Once a week, one member will take their interview notes on a particular member within their group and present this to the entire club.

3. Each week or month the group will have a guest speaker from the local business community as well as entrepreneurs. The guest speakers will talk about their particular industry; and their life leading up to obtaining their career, in addition to the hurdles and pitfalls they faced throughout their journey. The idea is to present a true picture of what these children will be facing so when they confront a hurdle they will know it is just a stumbling block to overcome. The speakers should come from a diverse group to showcase their overcoming different types of

adversity. Coordination with the Future Business Leaders of America (FBLA) and/or the Distributive Education Clubs of America (DECA) in obtaining these speakers might be a consideration since the objectives overlap.

4. If at all possible, the speakers will volunteer to personally provide mentoring services for a given time. This also should be coordinated with FBLA and DECA as they already have a structure in place.

5. Once a month, a guest speaker from a college will be invited to talk about their degree programs. In addition, they will answer questions about professions and what it will take to break into that profession.

6. Other guest speakers will include athletes, musicians, artists, writers and other professions in which the club members are interested.

7. Guest speakers from professions that do not require a college degree should also be included giving the students a variety of options for their future.

8. All guest appearances will be videotaped for future viewing if possible. All guest appearances will be followed by a discussion among the club members with emphasis on any questions they still have and what they gleaned from the discussion.

9. Club members will be expected to pick a career which may or may not be one they will ultimately pursue. They will be given

information as to expected annual income and will be required to prepare a budget of expenses based on their expected income. As a part of this, they will be expected to research the costs of apartments, food, gasoline, electricity, water, cable, insurance and any other fixed costs they might need to cover. The schools business teacher should be a good resource on how to structure and present this information.

10. A discussion of colleges, college costs and the basics of the student loan program will be given. This subject can be presented by guest speakers from colleges, your school's financial aid office, banks, and others.

11. Club members should be given the opportunity to run the meetings or to run their particular pocket group. This will test their leadership skills, boost self-confidence, and better prepare the student for life after high school.

Unpopular children are at a disadvantage when compared with other students and this club will at least level the playing field and hopefully give them a leg up over the other students. I envision the popularity of this club will eclipse all other clubs and the popular children will be begging to be members. Once this happens, the club will morph into an all-inclusive club with the goal of bringing all students together in a non-threatening atmosphere resulting in better attendance at school, higher grade point averages and a happy, well-adjusted youth population.

COLLEGE EDUCATION

Does a degree from Harvard differ from an online degree from the University of Phoenix or a degree from any other school? Is a degree viewed by a company as just a degree or are degrees viewed differently? Does the information learned at one school the same as another? Are different schools preparing students better for their career than others? If you spend $150,000 for a college education, will you do a better job in the business, scientific or academic world than a person spending $6,000 to get their degree?

These are questions that should and need to be asked. Since more and more companies are requiring college degrees, a better collaboration should exist between business and the educational system.

Reid Hoffman, an American entrepreneur, venture capitalist and co-founder of the extremely popular LinkedIn social network for business, has written a great article entitled "Disrupting the Diploma" that details an alternative system to:[93]

•Assist businesses in finding qualified candidates.
•Continually showcase the skills and achievements of individuals in a structured framework.

The proposed system is revolutionary and presents a technologically advanced approach utilizing certification in the form of icons and badges to an outdated college system that has lost its meaning. Implementation will be very time consuming but can be done in stages if the higher education institutions and big business buy into the concept. It is a win for business, a win for the individual and a win for education.

SUGGESTIONS:

1. Dramatically reduce the U.S. Department of Education.
2. Focus on local control of education and fund accordingly.
3. Increase pay for elementary, middle school and high school teachers.
4. Change policy to fire teachers that do not teach.
5. Discover and develop a more effective plan to distribute best practices.
6. Institute the school voucher program in every state.
7. The Teachers Union should study and embrace the teaching techniques in charter schools in order to duplicate or exceed these results in the public school system.
8. Utilize new techniques like Sal Khan videos to engage the students.

9. Have other teachers or the principle wear an ear piece and offer suggestions to assist the teacher in getting through to the students.
10. Bring fun back to learning.
11. Increase the hours that students attend school.
12. Change the college curricula to include advanced techniques for potential teachers designed to facilitate student engagement and attaining better results.
13. Make school uniforms mandatory for middle and high school.
14. Develop a club to include students that are not included.

CHAPTER 4

WELFARE REFORM

"I am for doing good to the poor, but...I think the best way of doing good to the poor, is not making them easy in poverty, but leading or driving them out of it. I observed...that the more public provisions were made for the poor, the less they provided for themselves, and of course became poorer. And, on the contrary, the less was done for them, the more they did for themselves, and became richer."
— Benjamin Franklin[94]

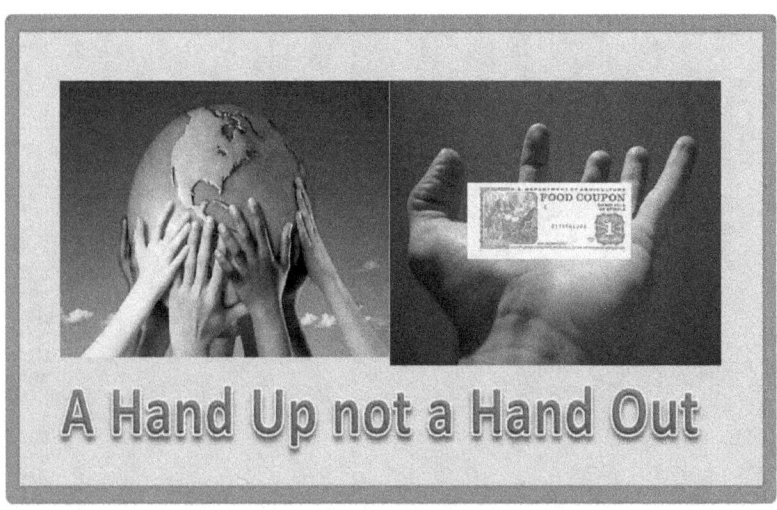

95

Welfare spending is the fastest growing sector of Federal Government spending which amounts to over 700 billion dollars a year including food stamps and unemployment benefits[96]. This total does not include the funding from the individual states. As a matter of fact, there are several states where a person receiving welfare benefits can make more money being on welfare than the average teacher's salary[97]. In a few states, welfare pays more than an hourly wage of $12[98]. When the welfare system proves that it is more lucrative to be on welfare than to work, this creates a huge, unsustainable problem. Why would someone get a job when they can make more money sitting at home? From a purely monetary standpoint, it does not make sense to work when you can sit at home and make more money. The more money the Federal Government keeps throwing at the problem, the worse it gets.

Our welfare system is like a drug. It draws you in with offers of hope and assistance and once you get hooked, there is no real program or incentive to get you out. There is virtually no incentive to work. A middle class family on welfare is entitled to many, many assistance programs and can earn as much or more on the programs than they can with a job[99]. Common sense dictates that the way to fix the system is to provide incentives to get out of the system and disincentives to stay in the system. Welfare should promote self-sufficiency instead of government dependency.

It is true that the welfare programs are now administered by the states with the bulk of the funding coming from the Federal Government and the states providing matching funds. Having the states control the programs is the right use of the funds but there is still too much influence from the Federal Government on how the money should be used[100].

There are over 80 various welfare programs providing cash, food, housing, medical care, social services, training and targeted education aid to poor and low-income Americans.[101] All of these programs require a staff of administrative personnel, technology resources, office space, supplies, etc. which are funded by taxpayer money that does not help the poor and disadvantaged. It's just overhead. Common sense says more money should go to helping the poor rather than paying for administration of all these programs. Approximately 80 programs should be combined into the following five programs: Cash, Housing, Food, Social Services, and Training/ Education. Medical care should be incorporated into the Medicaid program.

In the past, being on food stamps carried a stigma. People were ashamed they needed help from the government. They did not want anyone to know they could not make ends meet on their own. It was pride and the fact that they could not hide being on welfare from their friends and neighbors. Times have certainly changed. The current welfare system removes the stigma and keeps anyone from knowing you are getting assistance. You can virtually hide it from everyone although the fact of the matter is, they tell everyone. Welfare recipients even help their friends and neighbors with the ins and outs of the system and encourage them to sign up.

I was in Costco the other day and I overheard a woman on her cell phone telling someone the particular welfare benefits she currently receives and the benefits she is in the process of applying for. I was fascinated so I continued to slowly follow her up and down the aisles. She went on to explain how this person could also receive benefits and then offered to help her with her applications. All the while, this woman was pushing a cart loaded with food. The point of this story is this woman was not ashamed at all for taking taxpayer money but actually proud of how she was able to negotiate the system.

Changing the name of the program to Supplemental Nutrition Assistance Program or SNAP does not change the fact this is food stamps. Here is a quote from the USDA website about the program: *"SNAP offers nutrition assistance to millions of eligible, low-income individuals and families and provides economic benefits to communities."*[102] The government views the program as a permanent supplement not as a temporary measure to help individuals during hard times. As a matter of fact, nearly forty percent of the recipients live in households with earnings[103]. There are no plans to assist individuals to wean themselves from SNAP.

With this being the case, the program will only get costlier to the American taxpayer as time goes by. Do we really want SNAP to be a permanent assistance program for Americans? What message does this send to the American people especially our youth? Common sense says that this should be a temporary assistance program not a lifestyle. We should be promoting self-reliance and self-responsibility not government dependency.

Don't get me wrong, I understand the necessity for welfare and how it helps families when times are tough. However, I do not understand the current system and how it has no real path for getting families back to living on-their-own. In fact, our current system seems to encourage people to go on government assistance and stay on government assistance[104].

By taking away the original 'food stamps' and instituting the Electronic Benefit Transfer (EBT) card, there is no stigma anymore and it is no longer evident that a person is on food stamps when the card is used.[105] However, the EBT card system is wrought with fraud and abuse[106]. Companies are making a tremendous amount of money by issuing these cards.[107] Recipients are purchasing items that are not allowed like alcohol and cigarettes and they are letting others use their card which is also forbidden[108]. In many states like Connecticut, Arizona, Massachusetts, the recipients are allowed to get cash from ATMs which means they can then purchase alcohol, cigarettes and even drugs with the taxpayer's money.

This fraud and abuse is costing the American taxpayers billions of dollars.[109] Just the trafficking of benefits, defined as SNAP recipients selling their benefits for cash, has increased to an estimated $858 million annually.[110] This has increased from $330 million annually in the 2006-2008 timeframe.[111] About 10.5% of all authorized SNAP stores engaged in trafficking.[112] Arizona just made the largest seizure related to food stamp fraud in their history.[113]

Common sense dictates that the U.S. institute much stricter penalties for fraud and abuse not only on the institutions that participate in this fraud but on the card holders themselves. One offense for a recipient should result in their loss of benefits for a specified period of time. One offense for a vendor should result in a revocation of the establishment's privilege to accept the EBT card plus a monetary fine.

With all of this welfare fraud going on around the U.S., there must be many people witnessing this abuse every day. If you have witnessed welfare fraud and wish to report it, here is how to proceed:

1. **Make sure you have proof of welfare fraud** – In many states, you must supply your name along with the information so be prepared to vouch for all the evidence you provide. Remember, it is illegal to submit

false claims of welfare fraud so make sure you get all the facts.

2. **Gather the proof** – Write down the pertinent information including the time, date, parties involved, other witnesses, and contact information. Pictures or videos of the illegal event would be helpful but only if there is no risk of harm to yourself or others. The more information and proof that you obtain, the more likely the authorities will follow up on the case and cut down on this fraud and abuse.

3. **Find the contact information for your state** – Since the welfare programs are run by the individual states, each state has a different process on reporting fraud and abuse. For information about your particular state, contact the United Council on Welfare Fraud at http://www.ucowf.net/index.php?option=com_content&view=article&id=107&Itemid=65

4. **Write a report detailing the potential fraud** – Utilizing your detailed notes taken at the time of the incident; write a factual account of what occurred, not an emotional account. Sign and date the report and include your contact information.

5. **Submit your report according to the rules in your particular state** – Some states have hotlines to report welfare fraud

and abuse and some have mailing addresses, email addresses or websites.

6. **Once you submit the information, do not contact the state agency again** – Since welfare fraud is a criminal offense, the agency will not release any information concerning ongoing cases. However, the agency may contact you for additional information.

Americans must create a way out of this downward spiral. Jobs are the answer. The only way this situation is going to change is if government works with private enterprise to make this happen. If there is no transition path from welfare back to the labor force, families will continue to rely on welfare and this way of life will be passed on to future generations.[114] This is commonly referred to as the 'cycle of poverty'.

Do you remember in school learning about the law of cause and effect? Everything happens for a reason and all actions have consequences. For example, poor diet and exercise habits result in poor health. Continuous uncontrolled spending will result in debt and money worries. Increased dependency on the government results in less government revenue, higher government spending, higher unemployment, and more dependency.

CAUSE and EFFECT

Increased Government Dependency		Higher Taxes, increased government spending, higher unemployment, growing debt, more government dependency, weaker country

Now, let's discuss what can be done to transition program recipients back into the labor force. One way to do this is to institute mandatory job training programs. I'm talking about job training that will lead to real jobs.

There are many, many Federal Government departments responsible for training that have overlapping responsibilities[115]. Redundancies within the departments should be identified resulting in a consolidation of departments and trainers. Then, assign the redundant trainers and staffers to develop and institute a mandatory job training program for welfare recipients. These training programs will work in conjunction with local businesses to upgrade the skills of the workers to those who are currently needed in the workplace. If people refuse to be retrained, then their benefits are terminated and they are not entitled to additional programs for their families.

In addition, common sense dictates that drug testing should be instituted for all recipients of government assistance. Mandatory drug testing is required for workers so why not for those receiving government assistance? Why should the American taxpayers pay for the drug habits of those receiving public money? Government assistance is supposed to pay for the essentials to get families back on their feet not pay for drugs. Granted, adding a drug testing program is going to cost the states money but it does make common sense. I suggest the states begin with random drug testing to assess the cost impact on their budget before attempting to expand the testing to all welfare recipients.

Jobs will give people back their dignity and pride. It will cause them to hold their heads up high again and be a positive role model for their children, family, friends, and neighbors. A combination of a good education and the abundance of private sector jobs will stop generational dependency on the government. We owe it to our fellow Americans to provide opportunities to exit the doldrums of poverty and create a life of which they can be proud. Remember, it is not the amount of money we spend, but the results we achieve that counts.

There are private for profit and non-profit companies that provide on-the-job training as well as job training opportunities[116]. Some of these programs have amazing results. These successful programs should be utilized as models for government training programs to get people back into the workforce.

SUGGESTIONS:

1. Provide incentives to leave the welfare programs rather than incentives to continue to receive government benefits.
2. Consolidate the welfare programs into five making the programs more efficient and easier to manage.
3. Phase out the EBT card and bring back traditional food stamps thus eliminating most of the fraud and abuse.
4. Institute stiffer penalties for those that abuse or defraud the system whether it is recipients or vendors.
5. Institute drug testing on a random basis as a start and provide counseling services to those that test positive.
6. Work with the private sector to develop best practices training programs and provide a transition back into the workforce.
7. Keep your eyes open and report incidences of welfare fraud.

CHAPTER 5

FEDERAL BUDGET

"You balance the budget by restraining the growth of government and encouraging the growth of the private sector." - **Mitt Romney**[117]

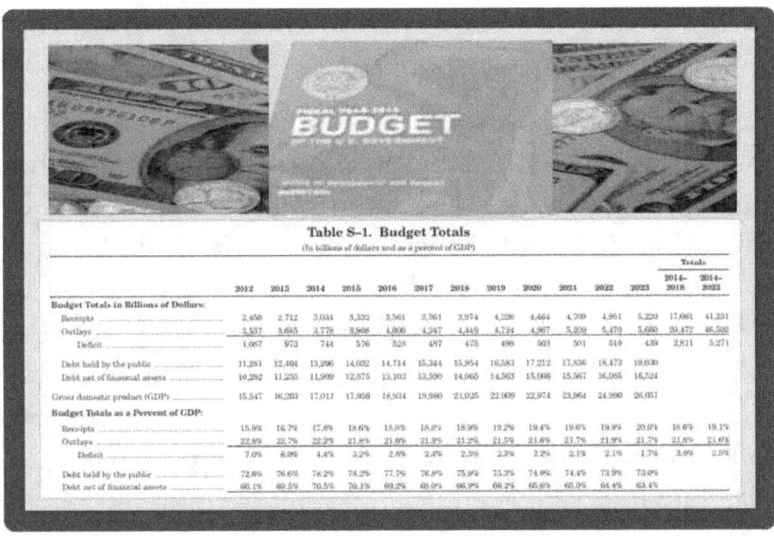

Table S-1. Budget Totals
(In billions of dollars and as a percent of GDP)

	2012	2013	2014	2015	2016	2017	2018	2019	2020	2021	2022	2023	Totals 2014-2018	Totals 2014-2023
Budget Totals in Billions of Dollars:														
Receipts	2,450	2,712	3,034	3,332	3,561	3,761	3,974	4,206	4,464	4,709	4,951	5,220	17,661	41,231
Outlays	3,537	3,685	3,778	3,908	4,090	4,247	4,449	4,724	4,967	5,209	5,479	5,660	39,472	46,502
Deficit	1,087	973	744	576	528	487	475	498	503	501	519	439	2,811	5,271
Debt held by the public	11,281	12,404	13,296	14,032	14,714	15,344	15,954	16,583	17,212	17,836	18,473	19,630		
Debt net of financial assets	10,282	11,255	11,999	12,875	13,103	13,590	14,065	14,563	15,006	15,567	16,065	16,524		
Gross domestic product (GDP)	15,547	16,203	17,011	17,956	18,934	19,980	21,025	22,009	22,974	23,964	24,990	26,051		
Budget Totals as a Percent of GDP:														
Receipts	15.8%	16.7%	17.8%	18.6%	18.8%	18.8%	18.9%	19.2%	19.4%	19.6%	19.8%	20.0%	18.6%	19.1%
Outlays	22.8%	22.7%	22.2%	21.8%	21.6%	21.3%	21.2%	21.5%	21.6%	21.7%	21.9%	21.7%	21.6%	21.4%
Deficit	7.0%	6.0%	4.4%	3.2%	2.8%	2.4%	2.3%	2.3%	2.2%	2.1%	2.1%	1.7%	3.0%	2.5%
Debt held by the public	72.6%	76.6%	78.2%	78.2%	77.7%	76.8%	75.9%	75.3%	74.9%	74.4%	73.9%	73.0%		
Debt net of financial assets	66.1%	69.5%	70.5%	70.1%	69.2%	68.0%	66.9%	66.2%	65.6%	65.0%	64.4%	63.4%		

By law, the President must submit a budget to Congress by February 1 of each year. From 2009 through 2013, President Obama has not complied by the due date. In addition, the Senate has not passed a budget since 2009. How can the Federal Government control spending or even know what is being spent if they have no budget?

I equate this to the average person's household budget. If a typical family does not have an itemized budget, they could spend or charge more money than they make without knowing it until it is too late. A typical family can only do this so long before their credit cards are maxed out. The government maxed out their credit card at 16.669 trillion dollars and had to get the limit raised. If the Federal Government knows what their expenditures will be via a passed budget, common sense says they are less apt to exceed the budget.

You might have heard politicians using words like 'investment' or 'investing in the future' when referring to education, infrastructure, etc. These are just alternative words for spending. If America 'invests' in education, it spends more money. The United States is "investing" over 30 billion dollars every month to pay the interest on its national debt.[118] In fact, the total interest expense on the outstanding debt for fiscal year 2013 was $415,688,781,248.40.[119] I suspect this money could be better spent by the private sector to create jobs.

CAUSE and EFFECT

Government Overspending Increased National Debt, Weaker Country

American politicians on both sides know how to spin the news into something beneficial to their particular political party. This does nothing to solve problems the U.S. faces and it is not what is desired or expected from American lawmakers. A little more truth and a lot less hype will make a world of difference.

While sequester was touted as something so terrible that the country would not possibly survive, it referred only to a reduction in future spending growth. To put this into perspective, the total reduction in future spending for sequestration in 2013 was 85.3 billion dollar out of over a trillion dollars of federal spending.[120] In subsequent years, the reduction in future spending growth is 109.3 billion dollars. This amounts to only 10.9% or a little over three months of interest expense.[121] If reducing future increases is such a problem, how is Congress ever going to balance the federal budget?

The two-year budget deal negotiated by House Budget Committee Chairman Paul Ryan and Senate Budget Committee Chairwoman Patty Murray in December 2013 provided for $68 billion in sequestration relief.[122] The sequestration cuts amounted to only one-third of the total sequestration during the next two years. This $68 billion will be added to the ever increasing national debt.

As of June 2011, there were about 2,000 top level .gov domains resulting in an estimated 24,000 government websites[123]. How can any organization manage this many domains much less the millions of pages associated with these domains? This is another indication of how the Federal Government is out of control and wasting the taxpayer's money. Common sense dictates that a government wide policy should have been instituted before they reached 50 domains.

How many databases does the Federal Government maintain? How much duplication is there between these databases? How much money is the government wasting by maintaining duplicate sets of data? As you might have noticed on your own computer, this can get out of hand very quickly if a central set of policies and procedures are not instituted and followed.

There are many government departments providing similar services and functions. Instead of analyzing the functions of each department and trying to consolidate functions, the American elected officials continue to increase the size of government. I must add one caveat, during President Obama's administration the number of federal employees actually went down. However, expenditures went up.[124] If you were to ask each department head what they could cut, they would come up with the same answer – nothing. Once a government department is created it is there forever whether it makes sense or not. To be fair, in the 20th century, Presidents have proposed eleven major government reorganizations. However, few of the recommendations have been followed due to either politics or the resulting consequences of the reorganizations.[125]

I have submitted many budgets in the private sector and have a good understanding of the budgeting process. One common theme I noticed was that budgets always go up. Never did we willingly reduce our spending because that meant we would have to reduce personnel and/or projects.

The business climate is in a constant state of change and companies realize that in order to compete, businesses must change with the times.[126] Every couple of years, we hired outside efficiency companies to come in and do an independent review to determine where we needed to reorganize, consolidate and cut. Reductions and consolidations were only accomplished by bringing in outside assistance from a team who could look at the problem objectively. It is very difficult to be objective when looking at your own department.

In addition, private sector companies instead of increasing the number of full time positions in the good times, opt to fill some of these positions with contractors. This makes it easier for the company to trim resources when times get tough.

This is exactly what the Federal Government needs to do. Common sense dictates that every Federal Government department should undergo an independent efficiency review to determine where it makes sense to consolidate, where it makes sense to cut and where it is prudent to reorganize. The Federal Government should also hire more contractors to fill positions of retiring government workers to provide more flexibility when economic conditions change.

In the private sector, companies routinely search for best practices both internally and externally in order to increase efficiency and maintain competitiveness. The Federal Government should take a lesson from the private sector and actively look for and encourage the usage of best practices.

Since the public sector does not have a profit motive, there is no incentive to cut. There is no compelling reason to reduce budgets and staff. You cannot fault the department managers as they all want to keep their jobs and keep the jobs of their employees. The best way to increase efficiency and effectiveness in the public sector is by integrating private sector policies.

I said the public sector has no incentive to cut which is not altogether true. While it is true there is no incentive *within* the department to cut, Congress has the power to reduce budgets, institute measures like sequester to reduce spending, and refuse to increase the national debt ceiling without conditions.

SUGGESTIONS:

1. Submit a budget on time according to the law.
2. Balance the budget by increasing efficiency and reducing fraud and abuse.
3. Conduct external audits of all departments and implement the findings.
4. Replace retiring government workers with contractors as feasible to provide more flexibility when conditions change.
5. Conduct a thorough review of all government domains and websites and implement the findings.
6. Institute a central set of policies to govern the use of technology including websites and databases.
7. Conduct a review of all government databases and implement the findings.
8. Look for and encourage the usage of best practices in the Federal Government to increase efficiency.

CHAPTER 6

NATIONAL DEBT

"America will never be destroyed from the outside. If we falter and lose our freedoms, it will be because we destroyed ourselves." **- Abraham Lincoln**[127]

At the time of this writing our national debt is over seventeen trillion dollars. That's

$17,345,693,600,744.[128]   This is over $150,520 per taxpayer or $54,637 per person.[129] A baby born today has over $54,000 worth of debt. It makes you think twice about bringing a little one into this world.

The national debt ceiling was $16.669 trillion until October 17, 2013 when Congress agreed on a temporary increase until February 7, 2014.[130] During the period from October 17, 2013 through February 7, 2014 there is no limit on the national debt. On February 7, 2014, the debt ceiling reset to the actual debt.

On Saturday, February 15, 2014, President Obama signed into law a measure to remove the national debt limit.[131] During the period from February 15, 2014 until March 15, 2015, the Treasury Department can borrow however much they need to fund the U.S. government without worrying about exceeding the debt ceiling because there is no debt ceiling. The U.S. government has been given a blank check to spend whatever the Congress appropriates.

The debt ceiling is supposed to be an opportunity to reassess prior spending and make corrections. Instead, it has become a heated battle over whether one party wants to shut down the government and one party wants to continue overspending. Both parties are wrong and no reassessment of prior decisions is being considered.   Both political parties have an obligation to the American people to act in a prudent manner and protect the money the Federal Government has appropriated from the taxpayers.

Common sense dictates that having a $17.3 trillion national debt is not prudent and must be addressed before it is too late and a solution is unattainable.[132] The time is now to make the drastic, political-suicide decisions for the benefit of the American people.

Congress has yet again kicked the proverbial can down the road until March 15, 2015. Instead of the Republicans contesting the debt limit increase and adding provisions, they decided to give the Democrats what they wanted. Was this the best strategy? Do we want our lawmakers to continue to spend money the U.S. government does not have without initiating a review of current government spending?

On April 10, 2013, President Obama said the following:[133]

> Obama, April 10: Over the past two years, I've signed legislation that will reduce our deficits by more than $2.5 trillion — more than two-thirds of it through spending cuts and the rest through asking the wealthiest Americans to begin paying their fair share. .... My budget will reduce our deficits by nearly another $2 trillion, so that all told we will have surpassed the goal of $4 trillion in deficit reduction that independent economists believe we need to stabilize our finances.

134

There is a difference between debt and deficit. Debt refers to the national debt and deficit refers to the yearly federal budget. Although the two terms refer to different things, they do have a relationship with each other. If there is a budget deficit, the national debt is increased by this deficit. Here is the real question: If President Obama has reduced our deficits, then why has the national debt increased 57% under his administration as of October 2013?[135]

The American people know the difference between reducing *actual* spending and reducing *proposed* spending. While the Obama administration has been adamant and upfront about their intentions to increase spending, they are partly funding this increase in spending by increasing taxes on the rich. If you 'cut' the increase in spending and call it a 'cut' and raise taxes and call it a deficit reduction, does this do anything to reduce the national debt?

Federal Government spending has been on the rise for the past thirteen years and it is not limited to one particular political party.[136] When George W. Bush was President, spending was through the roof.[137] The amount of the increase and the size of the national debt have brought this issue to a national security status. As of 2012, over 34% of the national debt is owned by foreign nations including China, United Kingdom, Saudi Arabia, Venezuela, Iran, Kuwait, as well as many others.[138]

An advisor to the Chinese Government and former chief economist for the World Bank wants a single global super-currency to replace the US dollar as the global reserve currency.[139] This would be devastating to the US economy. The world wants a reserve currency that is consistent and stable. Since the recent budget crisis, debt ceiling crisis, the $17 trillion national debt and the 2011 credit rating downgrade, the US dollar is losing its consistency and stability. If the US national debt was low and the economy was strong, this would never have been considered.

In 2013, the average monthly interest payment on the national debt of the United States is about 34 billion dollars a month. That's $34,000,000,000.[140] The interest rate is extremely low because the federal government has been keeping interest rates low since the financial crisis in 2007.[141] When interest rates increase just 1%, interest payments will increase by over 14 billion dollars a month. The aforementioned assumes a balanced budget and the national debt does not increase. Wouldn't you think lawmakers would do something about this? Wouldn't you think lawmakers would at least stop increasing the national debt by balancing the budget?

It is difficult to understand numbers so large and the future effects of increasing debt and increasing interest rates. The following chart is hypothetical but has a basis in fact with the following assumptions:

- The initial national debt utilized is $17.3 trillion.
- The national debt projections are based roughly on the Congressional Budget Office (CBO) deficit projections but on the conservative side averaging $500 billion per year.
- The projected interest rate assumes a one half percent increase per year.

- The projected combined interest rate is based on the 2013 combined interest rate for all security lengths.
- The projected average monthly interest payment is one twelfth of the yearly amount.

	2014	2015	2016	2017	2018
National Debt Projections (in Trillions)	17.8	18.3	18.8	19.3	19.8
Projected Interest Increase	0.50%	0.50%	0.50%	0.50%	0.50%
Projected Combined Interest Rate	2.474%	2.97%	3.47%	3.97%	4.47%
Total Projected Yearly Interest Payment	$ 440,372,000,000	$ 544,242,000,000	$ 653,112,000,000	$ 766,982,000,000	$ 885,852,000,000
Projected Average Monthly Interest Payment	$ 36,697,666,667	$ 45,353,500,000	$ 54,426,000,000	$ 63,915,166,667	$ 73,821,000,000

The hypothetical chart above shows the projected combined interest rate in 2014 to be 2.47% increasing to 4.47% in 2018. With this increase in debt and interest rate, the average monthly interest payments increase from $36.6 billion in 2014 to $73.8 billion in 2018. In 2018, over $880 billion will be required just to pay the interest payments on the debt. What happens if the interest rate goes up 1% per year and the debt increases by more than $500 billion per year which is the CBO projection for years 2017 and beyond?

This is unsustainable. America cannot keep spending with reckless abandon. In 2013, United States' revenues are expected to be the largest in history yet there is no balanced budget.[142]   America has a spending problem not a revenue problem and something needs to be done about it quickly. Have you heard the mainstream media talking about the national debt? Have you heard the mainstream media say that something needs to be done to reduce the national debt?

The bottom line is that American debt and monthly interest payments will increase until the United States government not only balances the budget, but has a surplus that can be used to begin paying down the debt. Just balancing the budget will not reduce the national debt or reduce the monthly interest obligation.   In fact, just because of rising interest rates, the monthly interest obligation will continue to rise even if the United States balances the budget.

What if President Obama raised taxes? This is what President Obama already did in 2013.   Congress passed a tax increase on the top income earners and now President Obama wants additional tax increases in his 2014 budget which will affect the rich and middle class.[143] Did you know the top ten percent of income earners paid over 70% of the total federal income tax collected in 2010?[144] I do not believe the rich have a problem paying more taxes. However, the rich want to know their tax dollars are being used wisely and efficiently.

Did you know there is a government website, http://www.treasurydirect.gov/govt/reports/pd/gift/gift.htm, where a United States citizen can elect to voluntarily gift money to the Federal Government to reduce the national debt? Apparently, this website has been around since 1996. As a matter of fact, in 2012 the gifts totaled over seven million dollars which was a record year.[145] An American can elect to make an inter vivo gift (transfer during a person's lifetime) or a testamentary transfer (a gift that takes effect upon death).[146] To me, it makes more sense to give the money to charity and let the government handle reducing the debt but to all those that want to gift money to the Federal Government, be my guest.

As to the National Debt, I am referring to the federal debt only which does not include any state or local debt. For your information, the middle class pays a proportionally larger share of state and local taxes because of the way these taxes are structured. The federal income tax is America's most progressive tax and thus is the reason the rich are burdened with paying most of the tax.

Is our auto industry better off since the bailout of General Motors (GM)? Would things be better if the free market system was left to do their work without government intervention? The taxpayers ended up losing about $10 billion from the GM bailout.[147] While it is true that American International Group (AIG) paid back the government for the money loaned to them in 2008, a bailout would not have been necessary had the government enforced the laws. AIG was allowed to get *too big to fail* by the government's failure to update and enforce the antitrust laws.[148]

These laws consisting of the Sherman Act of 1890, the Clayton Act of 1914 and the Federal Trade Commission Act of 1914 have been around for a very long time but need to be updated to keep up with the times.[149] The government choosing not to update and enforce the antitrust laws led to a breakdown of the system including forced government bailouts. Common sense dictates the Federal Government should do its job by revising and enforcing antitrust laws for the good of all Americans.

The American government has invested money in green energy companies that have gone bankrupt, one after another losing billions of the taxpayer's dollars.[150] There are companies in the private sector called venture capitalists. A venture capitalist's entire business model consists of funding startup companies like these. If these new green energy ventures are viable or at least have a chance of success, why can't venture capitalist firms fund them? This is the job of the private sector not the government.

Venture capitalists invest in risky ventures that may or may not succeed. That is their business model. In fact, venture capitalists companies have around a 25% success rate.[151] This means that 3 out of 4 companies they invest in go bankrupt or do not make any money. If venture capitalists do not believe the venture has a 25% chance of success then why should the United States government turn American's hard earned dollars to a venture that has a high probability of failure? This money could be better utilized. For instance, the money could be used to audit governmental departments and eliminate redundancy and waste.

SUGGESTIONS:

1. Reign in spending and balance the budget.
2. Let the private sector do what it does best. Let companies fail and no more bailouts.
3. Update and enforce the anti-trust laws
4. Do not waste the taxpayer's money and invest in risky, non-commercially viable ventures.
5. Update and enforce the antitrust laws.

CHAPTER 7

CRIME AND GUNS

"Poverty is the parent of revolution and crime."
— Aristotle[152]

There are no easy fixes to solving the violent crime problem in the United States. Do we outlaw knives? Do we outlaw guns? Do we outlaw vehicles? Do we outlaw baseball bats? What about hammers, wrenches, golf clubs, rocks, etc.? Where do we draw the line?

Is the problem the particular weapon or is it the person wielding the weapon? Are we producing a society of potential murderers? What are our children learning from violent video games, violent movies and music with perverse, objectifying lyrics? Common sense dictates that families need to scrutinize and pay more attention to what their children are watching and listening to because this has an effect on their development.

Why is violent crime increasing in the areas where the gun laws are the strongest?[153] As a matter of fact, guns save lives.[154] Common sense says only the law abiding public are complying with these laws not the criminals. If the proposed gun laws were in effect before the mass murders at Sandy Hook Elementary School in Newton, Connecticut, Century Movie Theater in Aurora, Colorado or Columbine High School in Littleton, Colorado, would the laws have prevented them? Will the proposed laws make a difference in gun deaths or will they just infringe on Americans 2nd Amendment rights?

America is a nation of gun owners and that is not going to change. Responsible gun owners do not purchase guns because they want to shoot someone. Other than for hunting and sport, gun owners purchase guns like they would an insurance policy. The gun is there when you need it but you really hope you will never need it. 95% of police officers never shoot their gun while on duty but they still carry them.[155] Guns are a deterrent and criminals know this.[156] I could not find any references for this but common sense dictates that criminals are reluctant to commit crimes if they know they could be shot which is why most criminals search for easy targets. This assumes the criminal is not acting spontaneously or under the influence of a controlled substance.

Gun laws are for law abiding citizens to follow. Criminals are going to get guns no matter how strict the laws are. They will not purchase a gun from a gun store and tolerate a required background check. They will steal the gun, buy it from another criminal or purchase the gun from a gun show that does not require a background check.

What are we teaching our youth that drives them to violence? How do we portray violence in movies and video games? How have military conflicts in Iraq and Afghanistan affected the psyche of the American youth? Has American society grown more violent in general? What is happening to law and order?

Another study should be conducted to explore the effect violence in movies, music, and video games have on American youth. Another study should be conducted that examines the correlation between poverty and the erosion of the two-parent household with violent crime in America. Both of these studies should be conducted by groups with no political or pre-set agenda in order to get an accurate picture as opposed to one plagued with biases against or for guns.

Does a person who lives in a secure high rise building in a low crime area need an AR 15 assault rifle? Are we trying to write laws to fit this type of situation? What about the family living on a ranch close to the Mexican border where drug smugglers and illegal aliens frequently cross the border? Can we dictate whether they need a gun or the type of gun to purchase? What about the single mother or the abused spouse? Do they have the right to protect themselves? The 2nd amendment of the Constitution protects the right of American citizens to bear arms but it does not stipulate the type of arms nor does it stipulate the specific characteristics of the firearms.[157]

Because the United States is made up of rural and urban areas, high-rises, farms, ranches, gated communities, lake properties, ocean front homes as well as many other dwelling types and surroundings, everyone may not require or want the same type of self-protection. However, the Constitution protects the rights for all citizens no matter where they live and what their surroundings are. If there are to be any type of gun laws, they need to be local and not state or federal. However, I am not advocating any type of gun restrictions. In fact, I do not need an AR-15 but I cannot speak for others whose situation is totally different from mine.

In addition to protection, there are the hunters and the sports enthusiasts. These people might live in a city where they do not need a rifle but they travel to other areas or other states to hunt. If localities institute strict gun laws, how will this affect the rights of these people to bear arms?

This is a very touchy subject that has 2nd amendment rights implications and is a non-partisan issue. The real problem is not having a centralized database that houses all the mentally disturbed and unstable individuals who should not own guns. In addition, there are no laws compelling a doctor to submit names of mentally disturbed patients to a centralized database. By requiring doctors to submit the names of their mental patients to a centralized database may deter mental patients, who happen to be gun owners, from seeking treatment. This is especially true of those that have served the country in the military and may be suffering from Post-traumatic stress disorder (PTSD).

There is no gun control legislation introduced that would have stopped the senseless killings at Sandy Hook Elementary School in Newton, Connecticut, at Century movie theater in Aurora, Colorado or Columbine High School in Littleton, Colorado. The proposed legislation is a symbolic gesture at best. Schools are gun-free zones as was the theater in Aurora, Colorado. Anyone who is going to go on a rampage and kill massive numbers of people will do so in one of these zones because they know there will be no opposition. Why give lunatics a place to commit mayhem? Apparently, these lunatics are cowards because they prey on people who cannot protect themselves. Common sense dictates that all schools have armed guards and scrutinize all visitors.

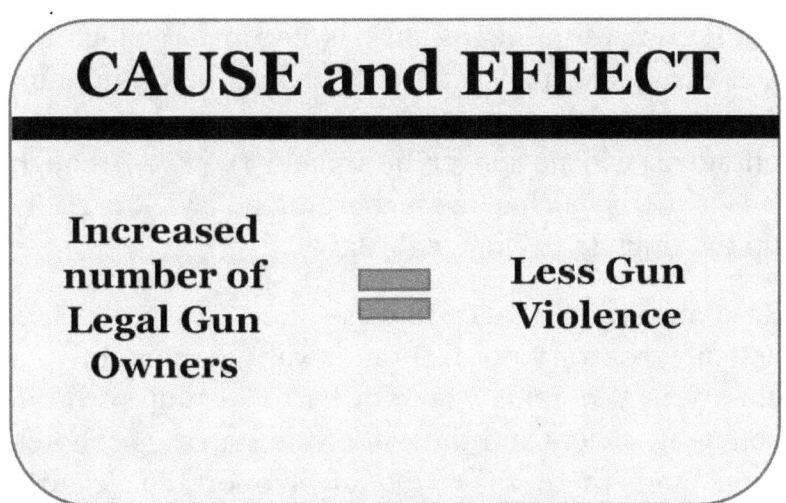

CAUSE and EFFECT

Increased number of Legal Gun Owners **=** Less Gun Violence

The focus should be on the senseless killings by knives and handguns happening every day in the inner cities. Common sense dictates that the areas with the highest incidence of violent crime be attacked first in a centralized manner.

More crime is occurring in low income areas where drugs and gangs are prevalent, where family units are incomplete, where education is not stressed, where children are not disciplined and where supervision in the home is minimal.[158] There have been no large scale discussions about fundamentally changing the environment the youth are exposed to so they have the opportunity to make intelligent choices about their life rather than follow a path to crime and drugs. The changes need to begin when the children are in grade school. Community support and outreach as well as local churches and synagogues should play a vital role in the development of our youth.

The Obama administration has begun to change the U.S. drug law policy so that mandatory minimum sentencing for certain non-violent, low level drug offenders will no longer be upheld[159]. Even though this is merely a change in 'charging policy', it is really up to Congress to change the law.

Several states now allow the use of marijuana which is actually contrary to federal law.[160] Apparently, a change in Federal law is in order to keep up with the changing society and the will of the states. Alcohol is legal and there is a lot of support to legalize marijuana. However, marijuana is a very different drug than alcohol. The equivalent of drunk-driving laws should be enacted as well as other considerations as to the location that marijuana smoking is allowed, the age requirement, etc. The big question is: Will a change in Federal drug policy help or hurt our youth?

Getting back to the crime problem, here is a possible solution. Create a federal anti-crime task force (FACT) to identify the problem, document proposed solutions and compile a detailed implementation plan. Tackle the worst area first and then move to other areas. Elite local law enforcement officers should be brought into the task force and taught methods and tactics, by FACT, to keep violent crime from escalating. Once a model has been developed and tested, law enforcement officers from other cities should then be added to the task force to work on the next high crime area.

The level of violent crime in certain cities should be a national issue. This issue should be afforded a high priority no matter the race, gender, or ethnicity of the perpetrators or victims. What is currently happening is not working. Until the severity of this problem is recognized and dealt with from a national level, a continued increase in violence is to be expected. The strictest gun laws can be enacted but criminals will still obtain guns and the problems will persist. Out of all the problems facing Americans, this one needs to be tackled now before it is too late.

SUGGESTIONS:

1. Families must pay more attention to what is influencing their children.
2. Develop a centralized mental health database to keep guns out of the hands of the mentally unstable, while being very careful of the significance of this database and potential abuses.
3. Provide armed security at the schools and scrutinize all visitors.
4. Develop a federal anti-crime task force to identify the problem, develop solutions, and establish an implementation plan.
5. Work with local law enforcement to implement the aforementioned plan focusing

on the highest crime areas first and moving from one area to another.

6. Once crime has been significantly reduced, establish a maintenance plan to deter reoccurrence.

7. Conduct a study on how violent movies, video games and offensive, distasteful musical lyrics affect the psyche of our youth and implement the findings.

8. Conduct a study on how poverty and the erosion of the two parent household have on violence in America and implement the findings.

CHAPTER 8

BIG BUSINESS AND UNIONS

"The greater the power, the more dangerous the abuse." **– Edmund Burke**[161]

BIG BUSINESS

Big business has been attacked for sending jobs overseas, paying executives exorbitant salaries, not hiring enough workers, getting tax breaks from the government, not paying workers enough, keeping their profits overseas as well as much, much more. Some criticisms of corporations may be valid while others are the result of massive governmental regulations.[162]

Let's first address the issue of corporations sending jobs overseas. American corporations are part of a global environment to which they not only compete with foreign corporations, but must compete with American corporations. Since corporations operate with a profit motive, it makes common sense to reduce operating costs to compete and stay viable. If a corporation cannot compete then it will go bankrupt and the employees will lose their jobs.

Why can't a corporation with American workers compete against one that employs foreign workers? Actually, American worker productivity is higher than other countries.[163] As you can see from the following graph, the U.S. ranks 16th for manufacturing compensation in terms of wages, pensions, benefits, and social insurance compared to the top 34 countries. China did not make the list as their manufacturing average compensation costs is less than $2.00.

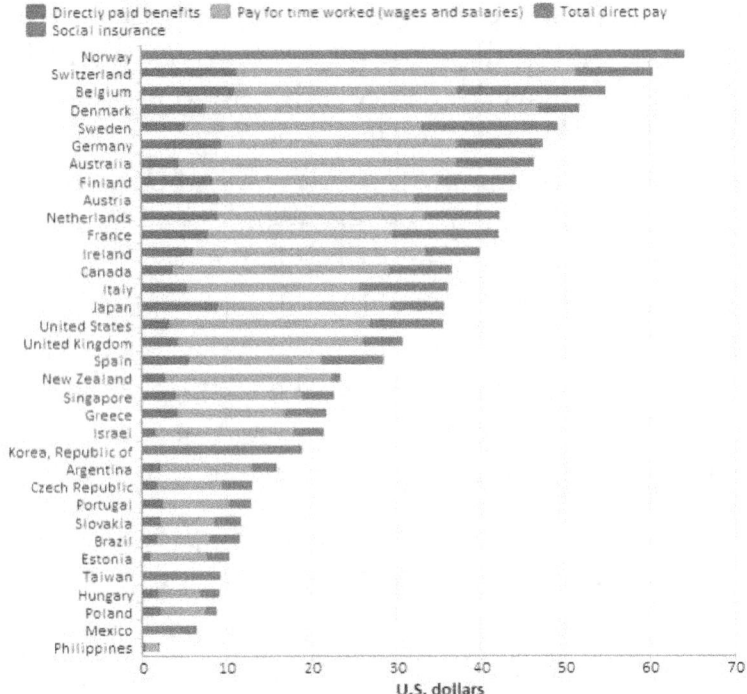

Manufacturing average hourly compensation costs in U.S. dollars, by components of compensation, 2011

Note: For Mexico, Republic of Korea, Norway, and Taiwan, pay for time worked and directly paid benefits are combined into total direct pay.

Source: U.S. Bureau of Labor Statistics, International Labor Comparisons.

164

Many people would argue that the salaries and benefits received by CEO's and upper management of many corporations are much too large compared to the average workers' salary.[165] Statistics show that the average CEO salary is more than 300 times the average workers' pay.[166]

While the CEO and upper management are highly compensated, CEO's and many upper management negotiate their salary, benefits, retirement and exit packages before they accept a job with a company. The company has the choice of hiring someone with a lower salary and benefits package.   However, corporations want a proven executive who will exhibit the leadership and drive necessary to enhance the competitiveness and effectiveness of the company. These proven leaders can either accept a position with an American owned company or take a job with a foreign-owned company. By choosing to work for a foreign-owned company, they will be competing against the American owned company.

The CEO of a corporation has many objectives. One is to increase the competitiveness of the company. Another is to create a mission and vision for the employees to follow. The third objective is to provide leadership and direction and build relationships. A fourth objective is to increase sales and enhance the company's longevity.[167]

Remember, I said that America is competing in a global environment? Whatever happens throughout the world has either a direct or an indirect effect on the U.S. economy.[168] This has been seen many times with the turmoil in Turkey, the fighting in Syria, the disruption of oil production in countries like Nigeria and Angola, as well as the economic problems with Greece. Global oil disruption or the prospect of lost global oil production causes a spike in the price of oil which has a far reaching effect on every facet of the U.S. economy. Countries with fiscal troubles cause an unsettling of the entire banking system and affect overall global trade.

Corporations have been sending jobs overseas for decades and by doing so, the standard of living has increased dramatically in those countries.[169] As the standard of living increases in those countries so do their wages, benefits and living conditions. Additionally, corporations have moved some of their operations from one country to another due to rising costs in that country. As global wages and benefits increase, it then makes sense to move operations back to the U.S. Subsequently, several corporations have moved their operations back to the United States such as Motorola Mobility, Nissan, General Electric and Caterpillar.[170] I suspect this will continue to happen at a more rapid pace in the near future.

Corporations have been knowingly or unknowingly raising the standards around the world, while decreasing the differences between producing products in the U.S. versus other countries.[171] It is a long process. However, the results have already been realized in many countries as some jobs have returned to the U.S. due to this very fact.[172] The American economy has suffered during this process, but as the process evolves, the American economy will greatly benefit.

The problem with corporations is that they have been allowed to get too big. The saying, *too big to fail* was a familiar phrase bantered around during the financial crisis of 2007-2008.[173] The antitrust laws regarding monopolies have not been enforced due to the exorbitant court costs, the political influence of the company, and the antiquated nature of the law.[174] Common sense dictates that Congress revise the antitrust laws to include *too big to fail* and then utilize the new law to break up these large entities before another crisis happens.

Apparently, nothing was learned from the financial crisis of 2007-2008 since American banks are still *too big to fail.* The U.S. government did institute additional regulation in the form of the Dodd Frank bill that, among other things, ends *too big to fail* bailouts for financial institutions but has done nothing to break up the financial institutions that caused the financial crisis in the first place.[175] The appearance of doing something does not mean the problem has been fixed. Action speaks louder than words.

We've discussed the macro problems with corporations so now let us drill down and focus on the employee. Let's face it; workers want the highest salary with the best benefit package available. This is only natural. However, when a company cannot compete in the global marketplace because of this constraint, something has to change.

Should the U.S. raise the minimum wage so those individuals being hired can make a living wage? My answer is no. Minimum wage is set by law. Generally it is the wage paid for entry-level positions in a company. Entry-level positions are intended to be just that; they are not envisioned to be careers. The free-enterprise system was designed such that a person starts with a company in an entry-level position, works hard, undergoes training and earns promotions to positions with increased responsibility resulting in associated increases in pay. The goal is to continue to move up the ladder into management and executive roles. This is how the system works. On the other hand, if a person chooses to do the bare minimum then they probably will not be moving up in the organization.

With respect to raising the minimum wage, any increase in the minimum wage will be passed on to the consumer in the form of higher prices for goods and services. The impact of raising the minimum wage is smaller for a larger corporation like Wal-Mart because it will only need to add a few cents to each product to recoup the difference due to volume sales. The losers in this situation are the small-to-medium sized companies who will be priced out of the market by the larger corporations and the fired or laid off workers. Fast food chains who rely on a large portion of minimum wage workers will suffer by reducing personnel and increasing the cost of their products. This will hurt the poor and middle-class the most.

Minimum wage should not be controlled at the federal level but at the state level. A minimum wage in New York City is very different than a minimum wage in

Panama City, Florida. Each state have different tax structures and cost of living which have an effect on the minimum wage.

Are employees in entry-level positions expected to work hard, continue to grow and take on more responsibility to demonstrate their abilities as potential candidates for higher level positions? Or, are these individuals expected to simply show up and do their job? If they just show up and do their job, which is perfectly fine then these employees are looking for an entry-level career. Companies have no trouble finding entry-level people to do the entry-level jobs. The people companies are really looking to hire are those who can be trained to handle positions with progressively more and more responsibility. This works in favor of both the employee and the employer in the long term.

You might complain that corporation management is making too much money and the salaries of the executives and upper management should be cut to provide more income and benefits for the lower levels. This is certainly a choice the Board of Directors could address and it may very well be valid. However, since the CEO has already negotiated an exit package, it might be more expensive to let the CEO go than to institute wholesale changes in the organization. Common sense dictates that while CEO's may be worth every penny of their lucrative packages, they also must be held accountable and risk losing all or a portion of their benefits if warranted by their performance or lack thereof. This is the missing piece and a major reason why the 99% are disheartened with large corporations.[176] If the workforce knew the CEO was risking his job and benefits then they would be more apt to accept their lucrative salary and benefit packages. Apple is one company that has made changes to executive compensation by placing a portion of their stock options *at risk*.[177] While this change by Apple should be applauded, it is not enough to only place stock options *at risk*. Bonuses and lucrative exit packages should also be placed *at risk* providing further incentive for CEO's and other executives to maintain the corporations' welfare as their primary focus.

Middle and oftentimes upper management are usually the scape-goats when things go bad for a company. They risk everything if their division or department does not perform according to specific company metrics. These executives carry the stress home with them even when they are with their families. They do not have the luxury of leaving their troubles at the workplace. This is how the system should work for the CEO and other designated executives who have already negotiated exit packages. Anyone has the potential to earn a promotion into a management position, but not everyone wants the responsibility, the accountability and the constant headaches. The more risk one assumes, the more responsibility taken and the more remuneration received. This is how the American free-enterprise system works.

What about hedge fund managers? Some of these people make over a billion dollars a year.[178] This is outrageous and there is no reason or justification for it. No one is worth that much money no matter who they are. According to our free market system, the sky is the limit and that statement rings true in these cases. Common sense says there should be limits, if only self-imposed. I am not sure how to implement this without encroaching on the free market system but a dialogue needs to be started. Rightfully so, this is one area the 99% use to argue their case and the one area that is really indefensible.

UNIONS

What has hampered job growth in the U.S. other than the economy, foreign competition and increased government regulations? One is union management. Not all, but some. Hear me out first before you make a judgment.

This has nothing to do with union members but everything to do with union management. Without unions we would not have laws protecting workers from abuse and mistreatment. I am not saying unions are not necessary, that they do not serve a purpose or were not instrumental in framing our history. Simply put, focus has been lost by management of some of the largest unions.

Private sector unions have been losing members since the Taft-Hartley Act of 1947 which placed restrictions on the organizing activities of the unions.[179] On the other hand, as membership in private sector unions declined, membership in public sector unions prospered.[180]

Instead of focusing on the treatment of workers and workers' rights, union management is intent on gaining power.[181] They do this by investing in political campaigns supporting candidates that agree with their ideology as well as reaching out to other untapped industries.[182] When the primary goal of a union is to gain power which means increasing their membership, there is a fundamental flaw in the methodology. When a group has that much power whether the group is a corporation or a union; they think they can make the rules no matter the consequences. Something is definitely wrong if the only way to get people to vote in a union or to protect union rights is by resorting to threats, harassment or retaliation.[183]

Some, not all, of the management of the large unions have forgotten why they were employed in the first place. Actually, that is not exactly correct because unions hire people in positions like political director, legislative director and senior political strategist which should have nothing to do with the focus of the union but apparently does.[184] These union employees are employed to further the union effort by gaining political favor much like lobbyists. The first reason why unions have these particular positions is the rise in public sector union membership and second, the influence government can have to further the union agenda. 35% of the public sector workers are union members whereas; only 6.6% of the private sector workers are union members.[185]

Unions were initially established to tackle the unethical practices and despicable treatment of workers by certain corporations. Since then, several laws have been passed that address many of the workplace issues but, laws cannot control everything. I respect Unions for their training efforts and for providing their members representation. However, when their influence is utilized to increase union participation just to increase the power and influence of the union, then they have overstepped their boundaries. This is what gives unions a bad name.

Why are Unions marching in support of immigration reform when just a few years before they were dead against it?[186] Don't illegal immigrants take jobs from American union workers? Is it because union management sees this group of people as a means to increase the ranks of union workers and increase their power and influence? I hope that is not the case but highly suspect that the pursuit of increased control and power has something to do with it.

There has been a lot of talk about *right to work* states and why businesses in these states may be outperforming businesses in states where unions are more prevalent. Common sense says that it should not matter whether the state is a *right to work* state or not. If companies with unions cannot compete with non-union companies, then the union needs to sit down with the company, analyze the discrepancies and devise a plan on how to increase competitiveness. This assumes that both union and non-union companies are treating their employees fairly. If a company with union workers cannot compete with non-union companies in their industry, then bankruptcy is the alternative. This is what happened to Hostess.[187] The unions would not agree to change their restrictive, inefficient practices so the company declared bankruptcy. This seems like an abuse of power and the union members are the ones who are suffering not the union management. When unions lose members, union management does not suffer. Hostess has since been purchased by another company and re-opened utilizing non-union workers.[188]

My first experience with unions was when I was working a part-time job on Friday and Saturday nights at a trucking company loading and unloading trucks. It was a union shop, but they hired non-union part-time workers to fill in during off peak hours. I was in the middle of unloading a truck and needed a forklift to remove a pallet. The forklift operator was on break so I hopped on the forklift, unloaded the pallet and put the forklift back. I was later called into the supervisor's office and told that the forklift operator went home. Apparently he got off break and saw that I was on his forklift and immediately called his union representative and went home. His issue was that he could not do his job because I was on the forklift. If I had seen him or if he had come up to me I would have relinquished the forklift to him with no problem. I just could not understand how he would just go home without coming to me first. This left a bad taste in my mouth for the unions because it did not make common sense.

As in the case of the Hostess Corporation, the unions required that certain products be segregated on trucks when it would have been more efficient and cost effective to combine products on the same truck.[189] It did not make common sense and appeared as if the union was instituting this process simply to assert its power. When unions work together with companies to increase efficiency, everyone wins. When unions work against the companies, everybody loses.

To me, union management should benefit when they lose members because companies are treating their employees well. In my eyes, that is a success and we all benefit. Unions are needed when a specific problem has been identified that is causing workers to be treated unfairly. Unions are not needed just to increase the influence and power of the union. Unions should complement corporations not work against them. Granted, unions are usually brought in by the employees when a company has failed its workers. However, in these cases, union presence should not be looked upon as a stab in the back to the corporation, but more of a helping hand and a wake-up call. In fact, because of the union threat, corporations have proactively instituted things like industry pay and benefit surveys to ensure workers are being treated fairly; hired an ombudsman to resolve worker conflicts and concerns in an impartial, confidential manner; instituted human resource programs to explain worker benefits and developed an inclusion attitude to bring employees and management together.

On February 14, 2014, the Volkswagen plant in Chattanooga, Tennessee voted on whether to unionize the plant or not. Volkswagen management is highly unionized in Germany and invited the UAW in to speak to their workers. In a vote of 712 to 626, the motion to unionize was defeated.[190] Apparently the workers were being well treated and feared that unionizing would have a detrimental effect on their great working environment. This should be a victory for Volkswagen, for the workers and for the union.

Have you ever heard anyone who is in a management position with a large union say they do not need to unionize a company because it treats its workers well? Neither have I. As I mentioned earlier, some union management has lost focus, but so have many corporations. Ethics and morals matter and when unions and corporations act ethically and responsibly, everyone benefits.

As a matter of fact, my son has been a member of a union for years and has taught me how useful a union can be when it is not overstepping its boundaries. Just like some power hungry corporate executives give corporations a bad name, the same thing is occurring in the union management arena. It is really sad that absolute power and greed have overshadowed truth, ethics and morality. Unfortunately, the average, hardworking employee is caught in the middle and suffers the most.

SUGGESTIONS:

1. Enforce the antitrust laws.
2. Revise the antitrust laws to include a provision for *too big to fail*.
3. Shareholders must be more vigilant and verbal concerning executive staff pay, benefits and accountability.
4. Bring back ethics and morals in business.
5. Corporations and unions should stay out of politics.
6. Union management should be held more accountable for their actions with union member money.
7. Union management should focus on the main reasons why they exist and not on simply increasing power and control.
8. Union members need to get more involved in what their management is doing with their money and vote out those who are abusing their privileges.
9. Union management should work together with corporations to achieve the objectives of both groups including increasing efficiency

and cost effectiveness while observing a safe environment.

CHAPTER 9

LOBBYISTS AND CONSTITUENT INFLUENCE

"Real lobbying reform must end the practice of corporate lobbyists writing our laws."
- Marty Meehan[191]

In simple terms, lobbyists are those who are employed to persuade legislators to vote for legislation that favors the lobbyist's employer. These employers could be organizations like the American Cancer Society, the Tobacco Institute, the legal lobby, etc. Some of the largest lobbyists groups are:[192]

- The Tech Lobby
- The Mining Industry
- The Defense Industry
- The Agribusiness Industry
- Big Oil
- The Financial Lobby
- Big Pharma
- The AARP
- The Pro-Israel Lobby
- The NRA

Are Lobbyists necessary? Do they reflect the views of the majority of Americans? Do they serve a purpose? Most people would say no, except when lobbyists are supporting a cause close to their heart. We elect our Congressman to enact laws. We don't elect lobbyists to influence legislation. Our lawmakers tend to forget what their constituents want when confronted with a suitcase full of money and a well thought-out argument. When lobbyists come between the voting public, it can have disastrous consequences. Lobbyists are good at spinning the truth and distorting the issues to make their case sound as if it is the will of the majority of Americans. This is how lobbyists make their living and they are really, really good at it. Common sense dictates that we outlaw the practice of lobbying. Let the voting public be the primary influencers.

Since lobbyists are so prevalent in Washington, town hall meetings have lost some enthusiasm. Negative press associated with interruptions from those with differing views also played a part in discouraging town hall meetings. I do not know of any district where everyone agrees with their representatives on all issues. Open, honest discussion of the pertinent issues is needed and all viewpoints should be represented. Will there be differing viewpoints? Yes. Will our representatives change the minds of those with differing views? Maybe and maybe not. Will our representatives get the feedback they need to properly represent their constituents? Yes, and this is what it is all about.

Our representatives should not shy away from confrontation but embrace it. They should not rely solely on the lobbyists to determine what their constituents want. Face-to-face, healthy, intellectual discussion of the pertinent issues will elicit differing opinions but it will also let the representatives know what is important to their constituents without a politically correct spin. Face-to-face contact is an important communication medium and should not be discounted because there might be confrontation. Many of these issues are very emotional to a lot of people and when these emotions come out, confrontation usually follows. I urge our elected representatives to just keep to the issues using truth and logic without getting emotionally attached to the outcome. In addition, elected representatives should coach their constituents on keeping the discussions at a logical, intellectual level and stick to the facts. Not just some of the facts but all of the facts.

Having outside political groups come to the town hall meetings with the purpose of disrupting the event should be met with severe consequences. If the people are constituents then they should be heard but not at the expense of the rest of the audience. Each voice has the same value. Groups who disrupt do a disservice to us all no matter to which political party they belong. Their disruption halts honest discussion with the objective of discontinuing the town hall meetings and thus stifling freedom of assembly and freedom of speech. Common sense dictates politics are politics but dirty politics have no business in politics. Truth is the eternal equalizer.

Technology has definitely brought the world closer together. Our politicians should make every day use of social media as well as other platforms to keep in touch with their constituents and identify the issues and top priorities affecting them. Businesses use technology to promote their businesses and also to solicit feedback to improve their products and services. President Obama is the first President to really embrace and promote technology in the public sector. Isn't it time our elected representatives in Congress do the same?

SUGGESTIONS:

1. Eliminate the practice of lobbying and institute stiff penalties for doing so.
2. Continue to utilize town hall meetings to get the face-to-face contact between representative and constituents.
3. Implement severe penalties for those who interrupt town hall meetings for the sole purpose of disrupting the meeting and presenting their political agenda.
4. Institute better ways of obtaining feedback from Congressional constituents including social media, webinars, emails, Web sites, online forums, YouTube videos, etc.

CHAPTER 10

VOTER RIGHTS

"Nobody will ever deprive the American people of the right to vote except the American people themselves and the only way they could do this is by not voting."

- Franklin D. Roosevelt[193]

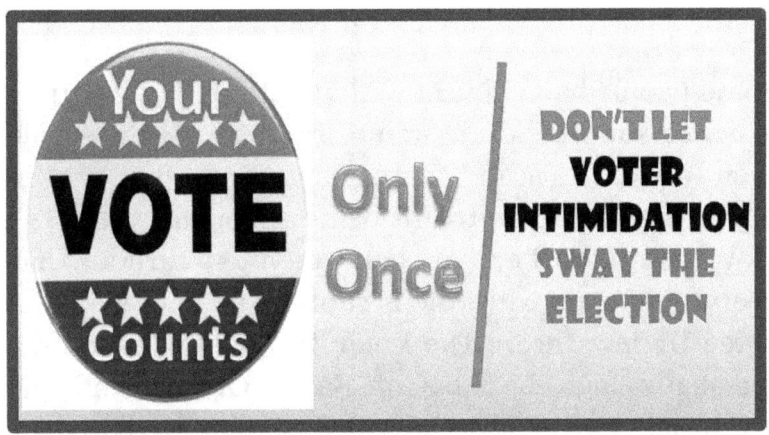

Every citizen has the right to vote and should not be impeded in any way from exercising this right. Having said this, every citizen has the right to one and only one vote. U.S. citizens do not have the right to vote for anyone else no matter the circumstance. How do you ensure that everyone has the opportunity to vote while ensuring that those casting a ballot have the right to do so?

If a person wants to cash a check or purchase alcohol, they must provide a form of picture ID and sometimes two. If a person wants to apply for government assistance, they must prove they are who they say they are. This should be the same for voting. This is not rocket science only common sense.

Why is it that some people do not want any kind of voter identification? Why are some people afraid of having voters identify themselves at the polls? Is it because they want people to vote for their ideology or are afraid that people will not? Do they want their political party to win no matter what?

Some people have indicated that voter ID laws equate to voter suppression of minorities[194]. If this is true then why did African Americans vote at a high rate in 2012 when compared with white American voters[195]? How can this be? I believe voter turnout has everything to do with who is running and not what the voter ID laws are. The voter turnout in 2008 was unusually high because of Barak Obama and the promised hope and change. Just like applying for welfare or Medicare or even cashing a check, people will find a way if the desire and motivation is there. Where there is a will, there is a way. If people want to vote, they will find a way. The real cause of low voter turnout is apathy[196].

Common sense dictates that every U.S. citizen prove who they are in order to cast their ballot. Whether this requires a picture ID or some other means to identify them, assurance is needed that voting privileges are not being abused by anyone.   Every American needs to know that their vote counts.

Even though federal law dictates who is a citizen, it is still up to the states to determine voter qualification.[197] Whatever they decide, there should be a plan in place on how to get all eligible voters an ID. This should be step one. It should be done prior to requiring mandatory ID's for voting. States can take a lesson from the mobile restaurant better known as the food truck. ID trucks could be dispatched to neighborhoods so residents who cannot get to an office can get an ID from these trucks. I suggest the ID truck have sufficient safeguards in place to prevent fraud and abuse. These ID trucks should be staffed with individuals not affiliated with any political party to avoid the appearance of impropriety.

Representatives from each state should come together to develop ideas on how to make this work without infringing on a voters rights. Since voter fraud has occurred in almost all federal elections, it appears that the penalty for voter fraud is not strong enough.[198] Common sense dictates that the penalties for voter fraud should be increased to reflect the seriousness of the crime. Intimidation as well as suppression should be prosecuted without regard to race, religion, sex or ethnicity. Every citizen is equal in the eyes of the voting booth.

Some people claim the instances of voter fraud are very small.[199] I suspect this is based on those that have been caught. What about the person or group that seeks out the names of shut-in people that do not have the means to get to a polling place to vote? What if these people or groups go to the polling places and vote in their place? What if these people completed absentee ballots for someone else and sent them in the mail? Who would know? Does this really matter? Are they doing anything wrong by voting multiple times? How would anyone know this was happening unless a requirement to produce some type of ID is instituted? How widespread is this?

In addition, the long lines at the polling places are another deterrent keeping many people from voting. In fairness to all, it should not take as long as it does to vote. Common sense tells us there is a better way to do it. Expanding the voting period and/or offering more early voting opportunities will increase the likelihood that eligible voters will have the opportunity to vote.

The U.S. men and women fighting for the freedoms of every U.S. citizen also deserve the right to vote. Extending the period for sending out absentee ballots should be considered so deployed military personnel have a chance to cast their ballot. Foreign deployments may involve periods with no communication with the outside world and thus require special considerations.

SUGGESTIONS:

1. Have the states come up with a plan to obtain an ID for all eligible voters.
2. Utilize ID trucks to sign up those voters who cannot travel to obtain an ID.
3. Require mandatory voter ID in all states to guard against voter fraud.
4. Increase penalties significantly for voter fraud.
5. Establish ways to expand early voting and/or increase the number of voting places.
6. Ensure military personnel are given adequate opportunity to vote given their unique circumstances serving their country.

CHAPTER 11

CONGRESSIONAL TERM LIMITS

"Asking an incumbent member of Congress to vote for (congressional) term limits is a bit like asking a chicken to vote for Colonel Sanders."
-- Congressman Bob Inglis[200]

In 1951, the 22nd amendment to the U.S. Constitution was ratified establishing in law the two-term limit for the Presidency.[201] Unfortunately, this only pertains to the Presidency not to Congress. Do you think the reason they did not extend this to the Congress was because it was the Congress that passed the law?

Generally, the average citizen does not pay much attention to their representatives and will vote based on the name they recognize from signs and TV ads. This is why many in Congress are still there after twenty or thirty years. Congressmen spend too much time campaigning and not enough time legislating. Congress was never meant to be a career. [202] It was designed for citizens to exercise their civic duty and fulfill a public service obligation and then return to their designated career.

During Congressional hearings, many of which are televised, do you wonder why Congressmen go into a diatribe and exhibit more than their share of grandstanding? It is because they have been provided a platform in which to showcase their skills and be seen as a concerned citizen looking out for the American people and the issues facing them? The real reason for the grandstanding is to obtain free advertisement for a re-election campaign and a boost to their ego. Common sense dictates Congress should ask specific, pointed specific questions, follow up with additional targeted questions, and let the respondents answer the questions. Additionally, when Congressmen follow up on questions they must not go off on tangents.

The United States is not the country it was 20 years ago, and Lawmakers must have up-to-date knowledge of technology as well as on-the-job business knowledge. A lawmaker cannot effectively create laws regulating small business if they do not have any experience working in or owning a small business.

Cyber-crime is a huge problem and reaches into all facets of American life from the economy, public health, national security as well as many other areas. Creating laws to thwart cyber-crime requires a specific knowledge of the potential threats that not all Congressmen have.

On the other hand, there are some advantages to having long-term Congressmen. Their wealth of experience serving the country and their knowledge of the legislative process can prove quite valuable. By staggering elections, these advantages are partially answered. The current U.S. election process ensures all knowledge and expertise will not be sent out the door at the same time.

Common sense dictates term limits be instituted. Senators should be limited to two six-year terms and House Members to six two-year terms. Serving in Congress was designed for civic-minded Americans to give back and serve their country and twelve years of service is definitely enough time. Once a Congressman identifies his or her job as a career then; keeping said job is always in the forefront of his or her mind. This thinking has an effect on their future actions. A Congressman's focus then becomes what he or she can do to retain the job rather than what is best for the country. America needs elected officials who have varied backgrounds, ethnicities, and experiences in the private sector creating jobs or managing companies. They also must be technologically savvy. Since the U.S. is diverse and highly global-oriented, international travel and experience is also very helpful.

SUGGESTIONS:

1. During Congressional hearings, stick to the point and avoid grandstanding.
2. Institute Term Limits. Senators should have a maximum of two six-year terms.
3. Institute Term limits for members of the House of Representatives. Representatives should have a maximum of six two-year terms.

CHAPTER 12

IMMIGRATION REFORM

"It's impossible to walk a block in Miami, in Los Angeles, San Antonio without running into someone who is being deeply impacted by a broken legal immigration system." **- Marco Rubio**[203]

We have an illegal immigration problem! Any country with over 11 million illegal immigrants within its borders definitely has a problem.[204] This problem was created by the Federal Government by not enforcing the immigration laws (e.g. not securing the U.S. borders, not sending all illegal aliens back across the border every time they are caught, not keeping tabs on those individuals entering the country on legal visas, etc.) for years.[205] The Federal Government has created a massive problem that is so large the U.S. is forced to do something that would never have been considered if the problem was a small one.[206] Common sense dictates that immigration reform must be passed now; not because it is the right thing to do but because it has become a necessity due to the numbers of illegal immigrants. Once immigration reform is passed; it makes common sense to increase the penalties significantly for anyone violating the sovereignty of the United States.

The 14th Amendment section one of the U.S. Constitution established that any individual born in the United States has the right to citizenship even if the parents are not U.S. citizens.[207] This law was enacted to make permanent the Civil Rights law of 1866 which gave the right of citizenship to African American children born in the U.S.[208] Slavery has been abolished and the 14th amendment section one needs to be amended to apply only to babies born of U.S. citizens. If this is not done then the U.S. will continue to exacerbate the problem. Why should the U.S. allow someone to travel to America, be it on a visa, green card, vacation, or illegally, to have a baby who is now a US citizen? The U.S. has a backlog of legal immigrants going through the lengthy process of obtaining US citizenship through legal means, but the

U.S. will grant citizenship to any baby just by being born in the US? This is another example of the Federal Government allowing the system to be legally 'gamed'. What I mean by this is there are loopholes in the laws that allow these types of things to happen. These children have easy access to American public schools and jobs. When the children turn 21, they can sponsor their entire family to obtain green cards.[209] This does not make common sense and it is not fair to those immigrants who follow the rules to enter this country legally.

In China, they have a one child policy so wealthy Chinese women are coming to America to have additional children who are immediately given U.S. citizenship.[210] There are China-based agencies that charge about $25 thousand in fees to cover travel, medical, visa, housing, and other related expenses.[211] After giving birth, the mother and child with a U.S. passport, fly back to China. As a U.S. citizen, the child can later return and attend college paying U.S. tuition rates rather than foreign tuition rates which are sometimes a third of the foreign rate.[212]

What is to stop other countries like Russia from doing the same thing? Could a Russian couple have a baby in the U.S., take them back to Russia, and train them to be a spy? Could this happen with Muslims cultivating Islamic radicals? The U.S. has opened the door to all possibilities. Until this proverbial door is closed, the unexpected should be expected.

The first step to enacting meaningful immigration reform is to amend the 14th Amendment section one.[213] However, this is not an easy step. There are two ways to do this. Firstly, by a two-thirds majority vote in both the House of Representatives and the Senate. Secondly, by a constitutional convention called for by two-thirds of the State legislatures. None of the 27 amendments to the Constitution have been proposed by this second method so it is really up to Congress[214]. After attaining approval from two-thirds of the House and Senate, the bill moves to the states and must be ratified by three-fourths of the states (38 out of 50). I do not think Congress has discussed this due to the challenge revising the amendment proposes.

If this amendment is not revised, the U.S. will continue to grant citizenship to children born in this country to foreign nationals. With the 14th amendment as it currently stands, the US government is responsible for the problem by giving citizenship to babies born in the U.S. without regard to the legal citizenship of the parents and the rest of the family.[215] The government is part of the problem and immigration reform that does not include a revision to this amendment will not solve the problem.

The second step to enacting meaningful immigration reform is to secure the U.S. borders with up-to-date technology. This up-to-date technology will facilitate detecting tunnels, performing nighttime interdictions and controlling the thousands of miles of border remotely. Since many illegal immigrants entered the country legally, but overstay their visas, a better system of monitoring those individuals who choose to break the immigration laws is needed. The U.S. cannot effectively address immigration reform until it: 1) stops the flow across the border and 2) tracks those individuals who enter legally but stay in the country past their visa's expiration date.

The third step to enacting meaningful immigration reform is to determine the extent of the problem by documenting the number of illegal immigrants residing in the U.S. A figure of 11 million has been bantered about but it is not really known if the total is half this number or twice this number.[216] Once the baseline is established an accurate count of the illegal immigrants, who they are, and where they live can be ascertained.

Next, a new status is created that does not afford the illegal immigrants full rights of American citizenship like the right to vote, but it does put them on the path to obtaining citizenship in the future. This status would have very different provisions than a green card. Green card holders do not have to apply for U.S. citizenship and can remain green card holders for life. With this new status, there should be a provision where the individual must earn U.S. citizenship within a specified period of time or they will lose their status and be deported. In addition, the individual must pay taxes as if they were a U.S. citizen. Additional provisions for this new status should be agreed upon by Congress.

The next step is to revise the current, overly cumbersome legal immigration system which is not working. By removing the complexities in the process, working more closely with the private sector, and focusing on the needs and not the numbers, the legal immigration system will be more efficient and effective.

The U.S. educates thousands of immigrants. These same individuals return to their home countries armed with their newly acquired skills.[217] On the flip side, if America had a system that rewards and retains these highly skilled individuals, then the U.S. would benefit greatly in many ways. Common sense dictates that immigration should promote those who can help the country not those who are likely to be a burden.

The next step is to change how the government views and treats illegal immigrants. Currently, there is a government Web site www.welcometousa.gov that encourages immigrants to sign up for government benefits and provides all the information to do it in both English and Spanish.[218] The following is a quote from the Web site: "Depending on your immigration status, length of time in the United States, and income, you may be eligible for some federal benefit programs."[219] Why does the statement not say 'legal immigrants' instead of 'depending on your immigration status...?[220] The U.S. Government must enforce U.S. law. Any government Web sites should reflect the law and contain clear, precise language that cannot be misinterpreted.

All of the proposed solutions are a direct result of the huge problem that the U.S. is now facing. The U.S. is diagnosing the illness and not delving into the root causes of the problem.[221] Why do so many people want to cross the U.S. border from Mexico? There are issues with individuals illegally crossing the Canadian border into the United States, but the overall majority of illegal immigrants are crossing the Mexican border.[222]

No one has addressed the root of the immigration problem or even discussed it. Why does the U.S. have so many Hispanics risking their lives to cross the border and start a new life in the U.S.? I believe the root cause is a lack of good jobs in their home country, mainly Mexico, and a concern for their family's security.

The focus is on Mexico because most of the illegal immigrants are either from that country or utilize that country to cross the U.S. border illegally.[223] Do you think the U.S. would have a massive immigration problem if Mexico had a growing economy and a safe living and working environment?

A common sense idea would be for the U.S. to form a joint venture with Mexico. The goal of the venture would be to increase the economic outlook and security in Mexico. The U.S. could assemble a panel of business executives with experience in job creation.

This panel could work with their Mexican counterparts on increasing the job prospects in Mexico. In addition, an organized team of U.S. security specialists could work with their Mexican counterparts on the security concerns in Mexico. If the U.S. could increase the economic growth and outlook in Mexico as well as alleviate the security concerns, then this plan would have a significant impact on the immigration problem. This plan may result in many illegal immigrants fleeing to their own economically thriving nation.

If the real problem with illegal immigration is humanitarian, common sense would dictate that a solution that bolsters the economy and security in their home country would make more sense.[224] The topic is definitely worth thinking about and discussing with your elected representatives.

SUGGESTIONS:

1. Congress must act on revising the 14th amendment section one so only children born of U.S. citizens will automatically receive citizenship.[225]
2. Immigration reform must hinge on securing U.S. borders as a pre-requisite with a pre-defined set of criteria indicating success.
3. Enact a comprehensive review of the illegal immigrant problem. The review should determine the extent of the problem and

individual specifics (e.g. how many individuals, locations, age groups, etc.) of the individuals involved so that a comprehensive solution can be established.

4. Congress must institute non-partisan immigration reform with a path to citizenship. As a result current citizens should not be at a disadvantage. Felonies committed by illegal immigrants must be considered when determining whether an individual should be granted citizenship. The border patrol should not be restricted from doing their jobs.

5. Increase the penalties for those individuals who enter the U.S. illegally as well as those who remain in the U.S. past their visa expiration dates.

6. Revise the current immigration law to retain highly skilled and highly educated immigrants who can benefit the country as opposed to individuals who would be a drain on the U.S. economy.

7. Form a joint venture between American businesses and the Mexican government with the goal of establishing a plan to increase employment in Mexico.

8. Form a joint venture between American security specialists and the Mexican government with the purpose of reducing crime in Mexico.

CHAPTER 13

BORDER SECURITY

"It's the federal government's job to secure the border." - **Carly Fiorina**[226]

If you watch an episode of Border Wars on the National Geographic channel, you will see real depictions of what happens at the U.S. border.[227] That is, about what the average U.S. citizen knows with regard to the United States borders. What is not known is the problem. Mexican drug cartels, backed by an amazing amount of money, are financing thousands of people crossing America's southern border every day.[228] In addition, known terrorists are exploiting the lack of security in the United States, entering the U.S. illegally, and undetected.[229] Sections of the border between Canada and the United States are not monitored 24 hours a day and provide an opening for potential terrorists to enter the country.[230]

Physically securing the borders of the United States is not the only goal of border security.[231] It also includes immigrants who enter the U.S. legally with a required visa and then become illegal by staying past the visa expiration date.[232] Some foreigners enter the country on a student visa but there is no follow up to determine whether the individual ever attended school.[233] A better system of tracking is needed as these people make up a large number of the illegal immigrant population.[234] The current system is not working. Therefore, changes such as having them check in at certain intervals, assigning them a case sponsor, utilizing biometric identity verification, or creating an alternative means in which to keep track of them should be initiated. In addition, stricter penalties such as making it a felony to break an immigration law may deter immigrants from committing the crimes.

Secure borders should be a priority before the U.S. government addresses the issue of immigration reform. The first step in solving a problem is to identify the actual problem. Before immigration reform can be a reality, the deluge of illegal immigrants crossing the border must stop. Common sense tells us that all borders will never be 100% secured, but the U.S. can come pretty close.

There is virtually no legal risk to an immigrant illegally crossing the border into the U.S. If an individual is caught trying to cross the U.S. border illegally and has not committed a felony in the U.S., the worst case scenario for them is that they get sent back to their home country to try again. Immigrants do risk their lives crossing the border illegally but what keeps them from trying again and again? Ideally, cooperation between the Canadian and Mexican governments to enact stricter penalties for crossing a border illegally is needed. The U.S. is more likely to make an agreement with Canada than Mexico simply due to the volume. Moreover, the issue remains that more illegal aliens cross the Mexican border and the problem will still exist if an agreement is not made. The next best solution is to enact stricter laws for crossing the border illegally. Currently, it is only a misdemeanor to cross into the U.S. illegally for the first time.[235] Subsequent entries are classified as felonies.[236]

Incarceration in U.S. jails does not appear to be a deterrent as it is most likely a step up from the conditions that many of the illegal immigrants have been experiencing in their home country. If the U.S. government can strike an agreement with the Mexican and Canadian governments to enforce the laws and incarcerate those who are sent back over the border, then the United States might be able to secure its borders more effectively.

I know that the phrase *illegal immigrant* is not politically correct but it is a true representation of these people. These individuals have either entered the U.S. illegally or overstayed their visa. Whether they are young children or adults, they are immigrants.[237] If the U.S. government cannot admit the truth about the situation, then how is the problem going to be solved?

Common sense dictates that people should tell the truth. Instead of focusing on renaming this group of people in an effort to soften the appearance of the problem, the focus should be on solving the problem. The problem does not go away by changing the name from illegal immigrants to undocumented workers. Incidentally, how do other countries label their illegal immigrants and what are the penalties for crossing their border? Why is it that other countries have either the same or stricter immigration laws than the U.S., but they enforce them without criticism?[238] Constitutionally, the Federal Government is mandated under Article IV section 4 to secure the border and it is not being done sufficiently.[239]

What if the United States changed its immigration laws to be the same as that of Mexico?[240] Would that be a terrible thing? Why should the United States have laws that are less restrictive than neighboring countries? If you had a family member, friend, neighbor or colleague who was killed by a drunk driver, would you be motivated to speak out against drunk driving? What if the driver was an illegal immigrant? What if the driver was an illegal immigrant who had been convicted of a previous DUI or had previous felony arrests?

Securing the borders is an easy thing to do in theory, but in practice it is very difficult and even more difficult to enforce. You cannot help but feel empathy for the families that enter the United States illegally and the situation that led them to the choice of making a long, arduous, and treacherous journey to cross a border illegally. They had to ponder their decision pensively knowing the risks associated with such a long and expensive journey. However, it must be mentioned that any one of these immigrants might be entering the borders to do harm to U.S. citizens. These immigrants have not adhered to the normal immigration screening and thus no one knows the exact reason for their journey into the U.S. Whatever the reason, it is against the law and the U.S. should not make exceptions. It is unjust to pick and choose which laws to enforce.

Subsequently, the United States has a problem encompassing approximately 11 million illegal immigrants and it is too large a number to handle with current U.S. laws. The Federal Government created this problem by not enforcing the laws on the books.[241] Therefore, the U.S. government must deal with the issue not by enforcing the rule of law, but by praying on the emotions of the American people. This is neither the ideal situation nor the way the U.S. should conduct business but it is the result of not enforcing existing laws. This is a lesson that should be taken to heart.

SUGGESTIONS:

1. Secure U.S. borders.
2. Make illegal border crossings a felony.
3. Develop a plan to ensure that immigrants entering the country on temporary visas do not become illegal immigrants.
4. Make it a felony to remain in the U.S. past the expiration date on a visa.
5. Devise a system to keep track of the individuals entering the country on a visa.
6. Work with neighboring countries to elicit cooperation on enforcing immigration laws; such as incarcerating offenders.

CHAPTER 14

TAXES

"We contend that for a nation to try to tax itself into prosperity is like a man standing in a bucket and trying to lift himself up by the handle."
— **Winston Churchill**[242]

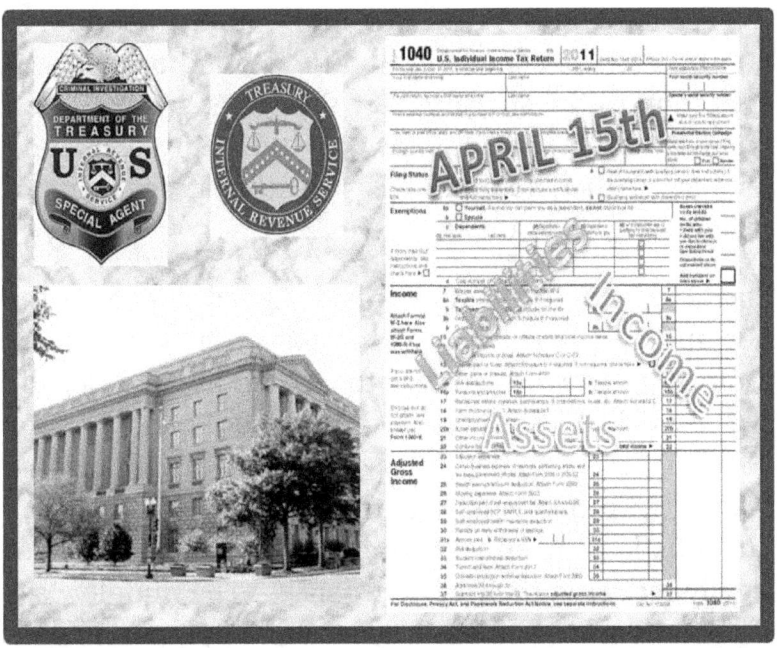

The current federal income tax code consists of over 73,000 pages[243]. No one can honestly say they understand all of it. It is bureaucracy at its finest.

The one advantage to having a lengthy tax code is the employment of thousands of IRS employees as well as over a million tax professionals, tax lawyers, and corporate employees responsible for tax compliance[244]. Employing this many people simply to comply with tax laws is inefficient, irresponsible, unmanageable, and unsustainable.

Adhering to all of the tax guidelines has a cost and the average taxpayer is the one who usually pays. Businesses have two ways of dealing with an increase in tax compliance costs. The first option is to pass on the costs to the consumer and the second option is to pass it on to the shareholder. Businesses usually add the cost of tax compliance to their products and services as they do other costs relating to government regulatory compliance[245].

The U.S. income tax system is designed to benefit the rich and the poor. The rich have the money to hire tax professionals who advise them on how to legally circumnavigate the laws. On the other hand, the poor do not make enough money to owe federal income taxes. As a result of this atrocity, many rich individuals own horse farms for the sole purpose of legally reducing their tax burden[246]. The middle class cannot afford to purchase farms and pay big money to tax professionals. Therefore, the middle class bear the brunt of the federal income tax system. Common sense dictates that this is unfair and should not be allowed to continue.

In addition, the U.S. corporate tax rates are the highest in the world.[247] As a result, Fortune 500 companies are reincorporating in foreign countries like Ireland where corporate taxes are much lower[248]. The current corporate tax laws are actually perpetuating this activity which results in reduced revenue to the U.S. government and increased revenue to foreign governments[249]. This is the reverse of what would happen if the corporate tax rates were lowered. Why not make America a more attractive place in which to locate a business rather than the opposite?

Common sense dictates that the current income tax system be scrapped and replaced with a flat (i.e. consumption) tax or a fair tax. Either system requires a thorough, in-depth analysis to determine which system is the best alternative to provide adequate tax revenue, market stability and continued job growth.

The fair or consumption Tax is a national sales tax that treats every person equally.[250] This tax is designed to provide the Federal Government with virtually the same amount of tax revenue as it currently receives[251]. Under this tax, every person living in the U.S. would pay a sales tax on purchases of new goods and services. Each state would collect the money, transfer it to the U.S. Treasury, and collect a fee for their efforts thus eliminating the IRS. As part of the fair tax, there would be a progressive program called a prebate[252]. This prebate would provide for an advance refund at the beginning of every month designed to prevent an unfair burden on the poor. There are many versions of the fair tax, but in essence the tax would eliminate:

- the individual income tax
- the alternative minimum tax (AMT)
- corporate and business income taxes
- capital gains taxes.

The main benefits of the fair tax are the elimination of the IRS, the reduction in compliance costs, and the ability for consumers to control the amount of tax they pay[253]. By consuming less, a taxpayer will pay less. As a caveat, speculation abounds that this rather large tax collected at the retail level may be doomed to fail due to a lack of retailer cooperation.

The flat tax is a tax system applied at a marginal rate to individuals and corporate income at a constant rate no matter the income amount[254]. The effect is a flattening of the tax base thus adding more taxpayers to the federal roles. Some plans counter this affect with deductions for lower income people thus turning the flat rate into a marginal rate.[255] The IRS would still exist so this would be merely a change to the current income tax system albeit substantially reducing personnel and complexity.

Debates continue about which tax system would be more beneficial to the middle class. Common sense dictates that a dialogue be started about replacing the current income tax system. A non-partisan independent study of alternatives to the current income tax system should be implemented and the results reviewed in a non-political, non-partisan fashion.

In addition, companies are hoarding billions of dollars overseas that could be put to work in the U.S. to increase employment and boost the U.S. economy.[256] Common sense dictates that the adverse tax consequences of moving money back to the U.S. should be removed.[257]

There are two schools of thought on this topic. The first is to revise the tax law making corporations pay U.S. taxes on money kept overseas[258]. The second is to drop all taxes on foreign money to allow corporations to bring money back to the U.S. on a tax-free basis[259]. The first option would raise a small amount of money for the federal government but, due to the current income tax system, corporations would find ways to legally circumvent the tax. The U.S. corporations in question would potentially come up with creative ways in which to avoid paying the new federal tax such as create and fund a foreign corporation using the tax money they should have paid to the IRS. The result would be a new tough tax with very little new revenue for the federal government and no money being brought back to the U.S. That would not be of much help nor is it what was envisioned with the new tax.

Option two is to let the corporations bring the money back tax-free. This option would not raise any direct tax revenue for the federal government. However, it would get the money back to the U.S. so it could be used to purchase property, expand and perhaps renovate existing structures, employ more workers, employ contracting companies, add money to the U.S. economy, etc. By having this money in the U.S., which amounts to billions of dollars, it could be put to good use which will result in indirect revenue for the Federal Government.[260]

As aforementioned, by trying to tax this money, companies will come up with creative ways in which to legally avoid paying the new tax. There are so many loopholes in the current income tax system and problems trying to gain agreement on tax changes in Congress that, the only real alternative is a brand new tax system.

SUGGESTIONS:

1. Conduct an independent review of new tax plans including a fair tax and a flat tax system.
2. Scrap the current tax system. Institute a new tax system where compliance is easy and possible fraud is either reduced or eradicated.
3. Remove the adverse tax consequences of corporations bringing back money to the U.S.
4. Provide incentives, in the new tax system, for companies to bring back operations and jobs to the U.S.

CHAPTER 15

ENTITLEMENT PROGRAMS

"By finding waste and abuse in entitlement programs, and eliminating it, we can ensure that the funds that are put into these programs go to the people that need them the most." **- Jim Ryun**[261]

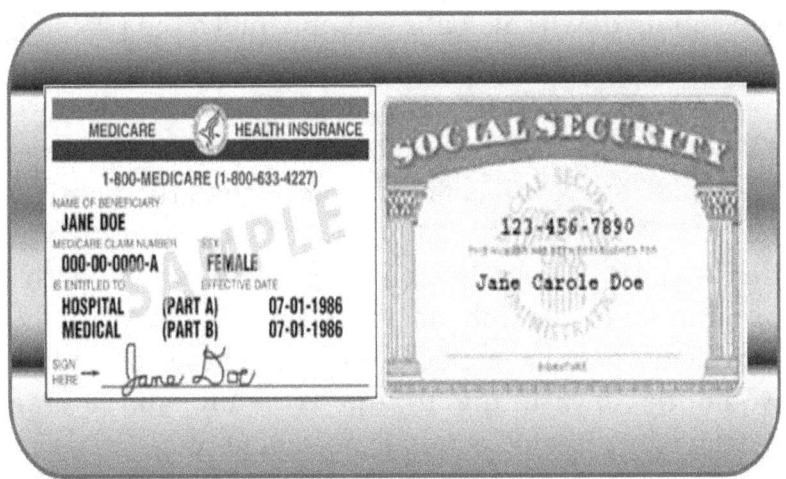

Entitlement programs provide individuals with personal financial benefits whenever the individual meets certain government stated eligibility conditions that are specified by the laws that authorized the programs. The most important of the entitlement programs are Social Security, Medicare, Medicaid, food stamps, unemployment compensation, most Veteran's Administration programs, federal employee and military retirement plans as well as agricultural price support programs. The welfare and food stamp programs are addressed in another chapter.

A good portion of the federal budget is allocated towards the aforementioned entitlement programs[262]. The unfunded liabilities in Social Security and Medicare are in the tens of trillions of dollars[263]. The amounts are too large for the average person to comprehend but common sense tells us that continuing down this path will only make the problem worse. There are potentially disastrous consequences to the actions taken by the Federal Government.[264] These consequences have been known for quite some time but Congress has failed to act due to the political fallout. There is only so long the U.S. can continue in this manner before the only option is to scrap the programs and default on the promises made to the American people. Defaulting on these programs would be devastating to the economy and is the reason why directed action is needed now.

The American people do not want these programs to go broke nor do they want them to stop. In addition, no one wants their benefits to be reduced. The ugly truth is that continuing to operate these programs without making changes is not an option. There are not enough rich people to cover the debt even if they are taxed at 100% of their income. The middle class is already overburdened so the answer is not to place a further burden on them.

In 1960 there were 4.9 workers for each social security beneficiary[265]. As of 2010, the number of workers for each social security beneficiary has gone down to 2.8[266]. The Congressional Budget Office (CBO) projects that by the year 2030, there will only be 1.9 workers for each social security beneficiary[267]. Obviously, this is a drastic change. The U.S. will not have enough workers paying into the system to support the increasing number of social security beneficiaries. To put this another way, in 2010 the total number of social security recipients was 54 million people[268]. This number is expected to increase to 91 million people in 2035[269]. Clearly, our current system which is significantly underfunded cannot sustain this drastic increase in recipients without instituting major changes to the system.

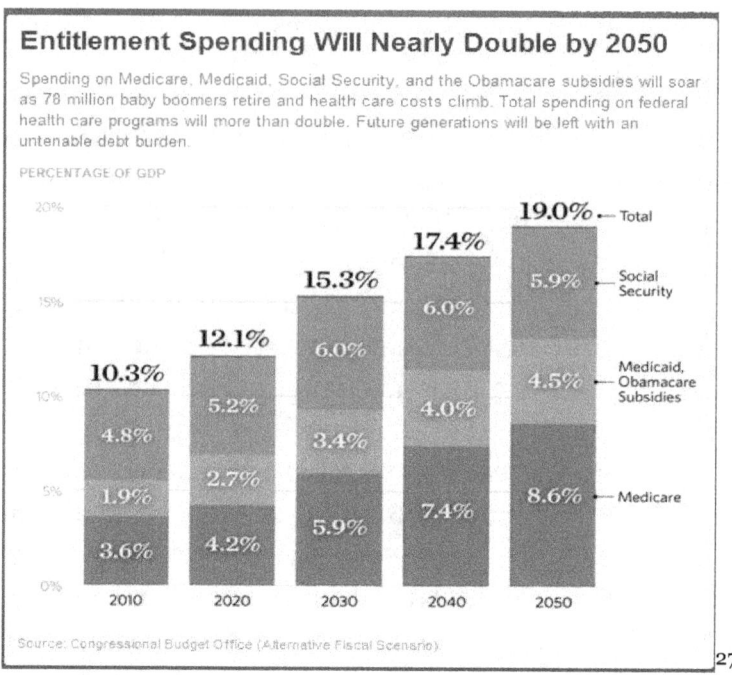

Entitlement Spending Will Nearly Double by 2050

Spending on Medicare, Medicaid, Social Security, and the Obamacare subsidies will soar as 78 million baby boomers retire and health care costs climb. Total spending on federal health care programs will more than double. Future generations will be left with an untenable debt burden.

PERCENTAGE OF GDP

Source: Congressional Budget Office (Alternative Fiscal Scenario)

270

The chart indicates, entitlement spending is increasing at a dramatic pace. Common sense dictates that a thorough analysis of the programs is undertaken resulting in a plan that will keep these programs solvent.

The truth of the matter is the population is aging which means that participation in these entitlement programs is only going to increase and increase rapidly[271]. With more and more people being eligible for some type of government assistance and fewer and fewer workers funding these programs, the outlook is not bright. Continuing to kick the proverbial can down the road is not an option. The only option is to address these issues now while there is still a chance to come to an amicable, long term solution. By waiting too long, there may not be an option to resuscitate these programs. If this happens, everyone will suffer the dire consequences especially those that are receiving these much needed benefits. The dire consequences are drastically cutting or eliminating benefits and a significant increase in taxes which will have calamitous economic effects.

Common sense dictates that two changes to social security be initiated:

1. Increase the normal retirement age of those less than 45 years of age to 70.
2. Raise the maximum taxable amount from $117,000 which is the 2014 rate, to $140,000.

When the economy is hurting, it is generally not a good idea to raise taxes but in this case raising the maximum taxable amount is justified. Social Security cost of living increase determinations should not be modified nor should other changes be made to the program to make the program solvent. It is a fact Americans are living longer and working longer anyway and thus increasing the regular retirement age is just a natural progression[272]. The alternative is to reduce benefits for current and future retirees. This decision would cause more problems than it is worth.

The Medicare/Medicaid issue is a more complex problem to solve. Since this issue is closely tied to the new Affordable Care Act, the full extent of the problem will not be known until the full implementation of universal healthcare has occurred.[273] In addition, the programs are wrought with fraud and abuse and thus addressing these problems is the first step[274]. Common sense dictates that an outside consulting firm be hired to conduct an audit of the Medicare/Medicaid programs. A possible payment option is to offer this consulting firm a small percentage of the fraud and abuse found thus costing the taxpayer nothing.

The Veteran's Administration (VA) has a vast number of programs for U.S. veterans. Some of these programs have the same characteristics as those for non-veterans. Subsequently, these programs are controlled and administered by the VA because the recipients are veterans. It makes sense to consolidate many of these programs. For instance, the Affordable Care Act should be amended to include healthcare for veterans. This action alone would reduce countless duplication of effort as well as personnel. Yes, some of the VA hospitals may need to be kept strictly for veterans. However, the majority of them can be consolidated with the ACA in addition to the majority of the VA health clinics. This is just one example where consolidation makes sense and could save the taxpayers money. There are many other such examples like employment, training programs, disability, life insurance, etc. that should be pursued as well. Common sense dictates that all Americans including veterans deserve to have the same care.

It may be political suicide in the short-term to address these problems but Congress must put politics aside and do the right thing. The problems are not going away. As a matter of fact, ignoring the problems only narrows the list of possible solutions until there are none.

SUGGESTIONS:

1. Revise the Social Security program by increasing the retirement age for those over 45 years of age to 70.
2. Revise the maximum taxable earnings for social security from $117,000 in 2014 to $140,000.
3. Conduct an external audit of the Medicare/Medicaid programs to reduce fraud and abuse. A percentage of the fraud and abuse found should be offered as payment to the auditing firm as compensation.
4. Conduct a complete review of the Veterans Administration in hopes of consolidating departments or activities in an effort to reduce duplication and costs.

CHAPTER 16

GOVERNMENT REGULATIONS

"A government big enough to give you everything you want, is big enough to take away everything you have." **-- Thomas Jefferson**[275]

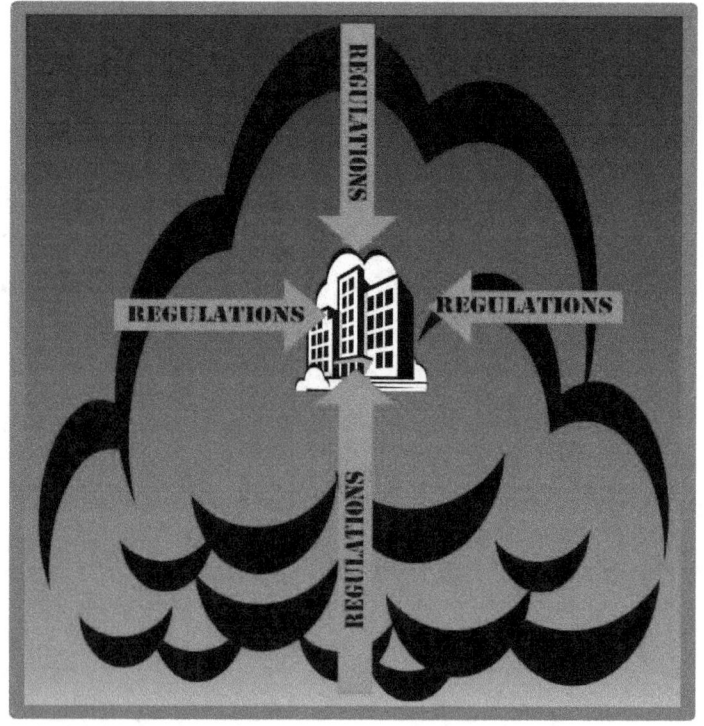

The only administration that reduced the size of the Federal Government in terms of the number of federal employees was that of Calvin Coolidge during the 1923 – 1929 time period.[276]   All other presidents including Ronald Reagan increased the number of federal employees.   The cycle has finally stopped during President Obama's administration with the help of the recession and the sequester.[277]   Even though the drop in employment numbers has been mainly due to attrition, it is a start.   What I do not understand is why this reduction did not happen sooner? Technology use has been increasing for years which would stand to reason why both private and public sector employment usually decreases.   While this has been the case in the private sector, it has not been in the federal government until now.   The U.S. government should have been systematically reducing personnel as the use of technology grew, but reducing the size of government has not been a priority given our history.

Can we really expect the number of government regulations to be reduced when we continue to operate with the same number of regulators?   What are these regulators to do but to create regulations? When has a review of all government regulations been conducted?   When has any U.S. President made it mandatory for all executive departments to go through, consolidate, and eliminate regulations that no longer apply or are harming business and economic growth?

In January 2011, President Obama detailed his plan to create a *21st-century regulatory system*.[278]   He also called for an unprecedented government-wide review of existing regulations.[279]   As a matter of fact, Presidents Ford, Carter, Reagan and Bush have all instituted regulatory reform by establishing agencies like the Regulatory Council, Office of Information and Regulatory Affairs (OIRA), Task Force on Regulatory Reform, Council on Competitiveness, and President Clinton's Reinventing Government Initiative which incorporated regulatory reform.[280]   What was the outcome of these reviews? There have been proposed changes but no actual results or impact on business. Common sense says that political gains will be made by communicating positive results from these initiatives.   If it is politically advantageous to communicate the results, why has the American public not been informed?

There are over 170,000 pages of federal government regulations.[281]   From 2009 to 2012, the federal government has issued over 13,000 new final rules. The public is affected by the cost of compliance which is estimated to be over a trillion and a half dollars a year[282]. That is an incredible amount just for compliance. To put it into perspective, the cost of compliance is almost as much as the total amount of all after-tax corporate profits.[283]

Most people would agree that society cannot function without regulations but are all of the existing regulations truly needed? How many are redundant? How many of them conflict with one another? How many regulations are inhibiting small business? Are new regulations really needed or are the regulators just trying to justify their jobs?

The regulatory process should include as one of the first steps to evaluate:

- whether other similar regulations exist,
- the estimated cost of compliance,
- the effect the proposed regulation would have on the economy, and
- the estimated number of lost jobs.

These results should be weighed against the positive aspects of the proposed regulation and should have a demonstrable influence on whether to keep the regulation in place or not.

The more government employees there are in the area of regulation and compliance, the more regulations will be written. Naturally, the government employees want to justify their positions and keep their jobs. The blame cannot be bestowed upon the employees for they are doing what they are being paid to do. This is not to insinuate that unneeded regulations are being created it is merely to suggest that more prudence in the process is required.

There is a way of keeping the regulators working without developing new regulations. Common sense dictates that the U.S. institute a moratorium on writing any new regulations. Those employees who were tasked with writing regulations should review all existing regulations instead. They should identify those regulations that are outdated or irrelevant and should be removed.

Over 50 federal agencies like the FDA, EPA and OSHA are called regulatory agencies. They are empowered to create and enforce regulations or rules. Whether you are a business or an individual, you could be fined, sanctioned, forced to close, and possibly incarcerated for violating federal regulations.

The regulation process is rather complex and involves publishing the new regulations in the Federal Register at least 30 days and sometimes more than 180 days before they take effect.[284] In addition, some regulations require one or more public hearings which increases the time period before the new regulations become law. The government has an obligation to answer citizen's questions, but this really will not affect whether the regulation takes effect. Once a regulation takes effect, it changes into a final rule; it is then printed in the Federal Register and the Code of Federal Regulations, and is usually posted on the Web site of the particular regulatory agency.[285]

With regards to enforcement, how many government regulations are being enforced fully or even selectively? The majority of Americans most likely do not know the answer to this question. How can the U.S. government have regulations that are only selectively enforced? Who decides which regulations to enforce? Are the penalties strict enough so people and companies will go to great lengths to comply rather than pay the penalty? Probably not. Common sense says to increase the penalties for the first offense and increase the severity for subsequent offenses.

Now that universal healthcare has been made available with over 18,000 pages of regulations, how can all of them ever be enforced?[286] How long will it take for businesses to hire the additional personnel needed and train all of their employees to adhere to the new regulations? As a matter of fact, the employer mandate which was scheduled to take effect as of January 1, 2014, has been delayed until January 1, 2015[287]. Common sense says that Obamacare is out of control and the legal system is the beneficiary. By establishing regulations with ambiguous language, the government has established the potential for different interpretations which may provide the legal community fodder for lawsuits costing taxpayers money.

The U.S. is a country of laws and the country cannot function at an optimum level if laws are not enforced. Once a government selects which laws and regulations to enforce, an increased risk of overburdening the court system is realized further reducing its credibility.

What about self-regulation of industries? In order to avoid more government regulations, industries would regulate themselves. Not simply enforcing government regulations, but establishing regulations by industry as well as enforcing them. This concept would be driven by ethics and morals on the part of corporate executives. It has happened in the past; it is happening today and is a great way of handling issues within an industry without having to burden companies with additional government regulations[288]. Furthermore, self-regulation may reduce the number of government regulations thus reducing the cost of government as well as reducing the cost of products and services. Imagine that!

The question arises as to who would regulate the corporate regulators? What about corporate greed, possible cover-ups, etc.? The great part about industry self-regulation is that if they do not do a good job of regulating themselves, that industry would lose the right to self-regulate and the government would take over the task. As corporations want less government involvement, it behooves them to make the self-regulation model work.

As a matter of fact, the Council of Better Business Bureaus (CBBB) has been working with world-class corporations concerning self-regulation since 1971 with very good results[289]. Their self-regulation programs validate the effectiveness in progressing the interests of both consumers and the business community as a reliable alternative to government regulations. With self-regulation, corporations need to demonstrate trustworthiness and responsiveness to both public and government concerns.

Common sense dictates that a moratorium on regulations be instituted as well as a complete review of the existing regulations in all federal government departments. As a result, a combination of government regulations and industry self-regulation along with stricter penalties for non-compliance appears to be a good approach.

SUGGESTIONS:

1. Declare a moratorium on regulation creation in all federal government departments.
2. Utilize the regulators to conduct a thorough review of all current regulations with recommendations to remove or consolidate unneeded, redundant or out-of-date regulations.
3. As the first step to regulation creation, conduct a review of the estimated economic effects including the cost of compliance and the possible loss of jobs. The resultant information should be weighed against positive aspects of proposed regulation to determine whether the regulation should continue.
4. Consider the language used in the regulation to avoid potential litigation.
5. Enforce existing regulations.
6. Increase penalties for non-compliance for the first offense as well as subsequent offenses.
7. Work with the business community and organizations like the Council to the Better Business Bureau (CBBB) to promote self-regulation in more industries with the result

being the removal of government regulations and a reduction of future regulations.

CHAPTER 17

ENERGY

"The fact that the price of gasoline has declined some in recent weeks must not allow Americans to be lulled into a false sense of security. Energy independence must rank along with border security as the top priorities of the United States." **- Virgil Goode**[290]

The Department of Energy Organization Act of 1977 created the Department of Energy mainly due to the oil crisis of 1973 and to combine various agencies[291]. Since the establishment of the Department of Energy, they have not produced an energy policy![292] Common sense says it should not take 35 years to create an energy policy. In all fairness, there have been the National Energy Conservation Policy Act signed in 1978, the Energy Policy Act of 1992, The Energy Policy Act of 2005 and the Energy Independence and Security Act of 2007 but none of these acts documented how and when the U.S. would be energy independent.[293] Naturally, one would assume that the Energy Independence and Security Act of 2007 would have contained something about energy independence but it was all about improving fuel economy, use of biofuels, improved standards for appliance and lighting and energy savings in buildings and industry.[294] While all of these things result in reduced usage of energy especially fossil fuels, it does not spell out how and when the U.S. will become energy independent. Simply coming up with ways to reduce fossil fuel usage, while a worthy effort, does not lead the U.S. to energy independence. As a matter of fact, these standards tend to increase the dependence on foreign made products in the short-term and reduce U.S. made products as manufacturing costs are still cheaper overseas. While overseas manufacturing costs are rising, the U.S. still cannot compete on price in most cases.

In 2000, China manufacturing wages averaged 52 cents per hour versus $16.61 in the U.S.[295] By 2015; manufacturing wages in China are expected to increase to $4.41 versus $26.06 in the U.S.[296] While the wages in China are still significantly below that of the average manufacturing wage in the U.S., this does not tell the whole story. Shipping costs have risen 71% due to higher oil prices and a reduction of ships and supply chain issues also have a bearing on the overall costs.[297]

People tend to have short memories and might not recall the 1973 oil embargo and the oil crisis of 1979 or the problems they caused.[298] By creating the Department of Energy, the U.S. has recognized that energy is important to the country; however, it has not been elevated to a national security issue to initiate the development of an overall plan for self-sufficiency.

This is a relatively easy problem to solve by using common sense. If the U.S. can satisfy all of its energy needs domestically or at least within North America, the U.S. can control the environmental concerns as well as control its own destiny. No more gas lines or gas shortages not to mention being independent of the Middle East. OPEC does not want the United States to expand the U.S. fracking efforts or to become energy independent as these efforts will hurt its main business.

Companies in the Middle East are financing feature films in the U.S. that advance their position.[299] Is this intentional or just a coincidence? It is not surprising that a country whose main source of revenue is in jeopardy; would stop at nothing to protect it. Is the downside of the U.S. becoming oil independent instability in the already tumultuous Middle East?

Common sense dictates that the U.S. approves the Keystone XL Pipeline as well as increase the number of available federal leases both onshore and offshore. By increasing U.S. oil exploration, employment will increase not only for oil industry jobs but also for the ancillary businesses not to mention the increase in federal and state tax revenue. The construction of the pipeline will add temporary construction and engineering jobs in the private sector, increase the tax revenue for the affected states as well as the Federal Government.[300] This should be a good thing whether it brings 50 jobs or 15,000 jobs. The U.S. should embrace all private sector job creation. The results of being less dependent on Middle East oil should override any other concerns. All of the environmental hurdles have been crossed and the endorsements have been received. The State Department issued their latest report on the Keystone XL pipeline in January 2014.[301] There is a 30 day public comment period after which the administration will make their final ruling.

U.S. oil production has risen in recent years as energy usage has decreased.[302] The increase in production is due to advances in drilling technology including deep water, fracking technology, and the availability of private or state owned land to explore.[303] The decrease in usage is largely due to the rise in unemployment and the increase in gasoline prices.[304]

In July 2013, the U.S. imported 306 million barrels of oil and sent $33 billion dollars overseas to support the economies of other countries.[305] Wouldn't this money be better spent in the U.S.?

Common sense dictates that as employment increases, energy demand will also increase. As energy demand increases, oil prices will rise if production does not increase accordingly. There is an abundance of federal and state land containing more than enough oil to satisfy the fossil fuel needs for generations to come if approval to drill on these federal and state lands could be attained. If the U.S. continues to allow OPEC to control the oil spigot, thus controlling the price of crude oil, the U.S. will continue to see increased oil prices which have far-reaching effects throughout the economy.

As of 2011, the U.S. has 104 nuclear reactors, 100 operational and 3 under construction, in 31 states producing 821 billion kWh making the U.S. the world's largest producer of nuclear power.[306] U.S. nuclear power accounts for more than 30% of worldwide nuclear power generation and over 19% of total U.S. electrical output.[307] Despite the almost 30 years of inactivity in nuclear plant construction due to the Three Mile Island incident in 1979, nuclear power continues to grow and be an integral part of the U.S.'s energy strategy.

As most people know, uranium is utilized in the production of nuclear weapons, to power nuclear power plants and with-in the medical and military arenas. The waste material from nuclear plants contains high levels of radiation[308]. Since the U.S. is the leader in nuclear energy production, they should also be the leader in finding alternatives for uranium.

Thorium is a radioactive chemical element that was discovered in 1828 by a Norwegian mineralogist Morten Thrane Esmark.[309] The element was actually named after the Norse god of thunder, Thor.[310] Thorium is more abundant than uranium and the U.S. actually has about 8% of the world's supply.[311] Even though thorium has been utilized as a nuclear fuel for 40 years, it still requires further testing.[312]

Norway built a thorium nuclear reactor in Halden, Norway which is currently being tested.[313] The reactor will operate for a period of 5 years after which a full analysis of the fuel will be conducted to determine if it is ready for commercial reactors.[314] Since thorium is safer and less messy to clean up, this may be the wave of the future for nuclear power.

Here is the bottom line, it just makes common sense to work diligently to attain energy independence and once achieved, pursue alternatives to fossil fuels. It does not make common sense to seek alternatives that are not commercially viable while still relying on foreign oil. If the U.S. controls its destiny by becoming energy independent, it can write its own ticket. The U.S. can then encourage and plan for decreasing fossil fuel usage and increase alternative fuel source development. If the U.S. does not attain energy independence first, it will continue to be at the mercy of the Middle East. It will only make the journey from fossil fuels that much more difficult, lengthy, and expensive. It is better and more efficient to function from a position of power and strength than a position of weakness. Power comes from independence whereas weakness comes from dependence.

The major oil companies have been heavily involved in developing alternative fuel sources for many, many years.[315] When the U.S. becomes energy self-sufficient and institutes a plan to migrate to alternative fuels, it will be the oil companies that lead the charge. Oil companies have the resources and connections overseas in places where it is commercially viable due to the already high cost of energy. However, this will not occur while the U.S. remains dependent on foreign oil and alternative fuel sources are not commercially viable. Offering government subsidies and tax credits does not make alternative fuels commercially viable.

As President Obama said, the U.S. needs an "all of the above strategy" to support its energy needs. However, common sense dictates that the strategy must be cost effective and commercially viable in the marketplace. Yes, other countries are ahead of the U.S. in alternative energy sources because they have been experiencing higher oil costs than the U.S. However, these alternative energy sources are not yet commercially viable in the U.S. It does not make common sense to increase the cost of energy just to introduce alternative energy sources. In this scenario, prices of goods and services will rise affecting the poor and middle class the most which will only cause further harm to the economy. The transition should be part of the National Energy Plan and begin once energy independence has been attained.

As with any new technology, costs are greatest in the beginning to develop the technology and integrate it into the mainstream.[316] Once the technology has been developed and deployed, companies entering the marketplace stand to benefit greatly. The government is actually harming startup companies by providing incentives to enter into a non-commercially viable marketplace because the risk of bankruptcy is greater than the risk of success.

The Federal Government must take a leadership role and provide both a short-term and long-term plan for their energy future. This plan should include a specific goal of achieving energy independence at a certain date. In addition, there should be a long-term plan to reduce the dependency on fossil fuels so companies can anticipate what is coming and plan accordingly. As it stands currently, no one knows what the future holds. Therefore, they cannot adequately plan for the future.

Corporations develop long-range business plans. Therefore, it would be advantageous to all if the Federal Government could work together with private enterprise to affect environmental as well as economic change. Everybody wins if government and business work together in concert to achieve the country's goals.

SUGGESTIONS:

1. Develop a comprehensive energy policy that includes a deadline as to when the U.S. will attain oil independence and a plan to move from fossil fuels to alternative fuels.
2. Approve the Keystone XL Pipeline.
3. Increase the number of available oil leases on federal land both onshore and offshore.
4. Increase fracking operations.
5. Provide a comprehensive review of thorium as an alternative to uranium.
6. Let the free market work and if alternative fuels are viable, let venture capital firms finance them instead of the Federal Government.

CHAPTER 18

ENVIRONMENTAL CONCERNS

"We do not inherit the earth from our ancestors; we borrow it from our children" – **Chief Seattle**[317]

Is America experiencing a climate change? Is it global warming or global cooling? Are humans to blame for the environmental climate shifts in our world? If there is an environmental problem does it need to be solved right now? There are plenty of scientists on hand who would agree whichever position a person held.[318] That does not make common sense. Science is supposed to be non-partisan so; why is there such a division and why do people get so upset when someone disagrees with their position? The reason for the division boils down to money. Whoever pays for the research controls the results whether the results are actual or written up to support a hypothesis given to scientists. This does not mean all science is tainted. However, this issue is a political hot button with enormous economic consequences, therefore, the possibility exists.

There are also those who believe in a cause because they want it to be true whether the science supports their position or not.[319] They are called zealots and appear in every facet of life. There is nothing that can be said or done to change their minds even if irrefutable scientific evidence exists.

In addition, there are scientists who believe global weather patterns are not affected by CO_2 emissions rather from an eleven-year cycle of solar sunspot activity in correlation with ocean temperatures coupled with other events like volcanic activity[320]. While solar sunspot activity, oceanic temperatures and volcanic activity have been collected for over 100 years, the methods and analytical tools continue to evolve resulting in more predictive capability.[321] Could this explain our climate change? This position seems interesting and worth pursuing.

There was an article in the UK Daily Mail that indicated there was a 60% increase in the total area of ocean covered with ice.[322] While this may or may not be true, the ice cap changes from year to year so this is not an indication of climate change. Utilizing data from an extended period of time will yield the best results. A leaked report from The United Nations Intergovernmental Panel on Climate Change (IPCC) revealed that the world is moving towards a period of cooling rather than warming which will last until the middle of the century.[323] Again, this may be speculation but the supporters of the IPCC's Fifth Assessment Report are requesting more than 1,500 changes to the report's summary for policymakers.[324] If scientists produce a report based on scientific facts, the only reason for demanding changes to the report by non-scientists is for clarity purposes. Revisions by individuals or companies funding the report for the purpose of skewing the results are unethical. The appearance of impropriety exists which leads to mistrust by the general public.

Is there a basis for climate change? Viewing the issue from a common sense perspective leads to the following four possible scenarios:

Scenario 1 - Climate change is real and the U.S. does nothing to address it

Climate change is real and the U.S. contributes to the problem. By ignoring the problem, the U.S. is perpetuating it. As things continue to deteriorate, it is only logical that the U.S. realize the issues at hand and do something. Whether global climate changes can be reversed remains to be seen.

Scenario 2 – Climate change is not real and the U.S. acts as if it exists

The U.S. is effectively increasing the cost of living but not the wages by reducing carbon emissions; moving away from fossil fuels; re-establishing forests, etc. Many long-standing businesses are now out of business, people are out of work because the companies they worked for are either no longer viable or have been forced to reduce employment. The U.S. is forced into alternative new ventures without going through the necessary incubation period. This leads to inefficiencies and uneconomical practices that would have worked themselves out in the real world over time.

New ventures will be up and running one day and bankrupt the next with taxpayers footing the bill for the startups and failures. The economy is in a shambles because it has put its trust in the new, untested startups while ruining established businesses. The government has increased its power and control by funding these new ventures. The reason being the new businesses are not commercially viable and thus no venture capital firm will want to fund such risky investments.

Scenario 3 – Climate change is real and the U.S. does everything it should

The U.S. is effectively in the same position as Scenario 2, but this time it has a purpose. Because no comprehensive Energy Plan exists and the business community has not been planning a move into alternative energy sources on a large scale, the U.S. is unprepared. Inefficiencies and uneconomical practices will result as well as increased prices. The economy will be turned upside down and suffer for a period until the ingenuity of the American people overcomes the adversity.

Scenario 4 – Climate change is not real and the U.S. does nothing

This is the best of all scenarios and the least costly. Is this a possibility?

Common sense dictates that when a problem is identified possible causes should be ascertained before potential solutions can be suggested. Because the world has politicized the science, it is difficult to determine whether an agreement on the problem is real. By remaining on the current path, there will be continued doubt in the minds of the public. If the different factions continue to fight amongst each other, agreement will never be obtained. Fear is a powerful motivator. However, spreading fear that a problem exists is not a reason to upset the American way of life and possibly do real harm to the economy. On the other hand, if the problem is real then the fear is valid and the U.S. will be playing catch-up.

The solution is to fund an independent group of scientists to work on the problem. These scientists should not be funded or influenced by any group, political party, or country that has a political, economic, or environmental motive which may have an effect on the outcome. This should not be a rushed study, but one that follows normal scientific principles and protocols. The solution is not to find answers to a hypothetical climate change problem, but to actually start with a clean slate and determine if there is anything other than nature that is having an effect on long-term climate patterns. If the results indicate that humans are having an effect on climate change, it is common sense to ascertain answers to the what, where, and why questions before affecting solutions.

If it is determined that climate change is real, the U.S. can then begin to develop a plan containing both long-term and short-term solutions to mitigate and/or resolve the problem in a non-political, non-partisan, economically-friendly fashion. If the problem is real, keep in mind the problem is a global one requiring commitment, support, and agreement from the rest of the world to affect viable worldwide solutions.

Having spent over a decade working in several different countries around the world, my experience has revealed that the U.S. is the most environmentally conscious country in the world. When I worked in Angola, West Africa, a U.S. based oil company wrote the environmental policy for the country. The U.S. Company had partners from Italy and France who did not want to implement such strict rules. The reason being the companies did not want their profits affected but eventually; complied. This is a little known fact that does not get much media attention because it is counter to the way the media views oil companies in general. In addition to writing the environmental policy, this U.S. Company also built schools and hospitals and provided medicine and supplies to the people.

It just makes common sense for the environmental efforts to focus on countries that are the worst polluters, China and the United States. Their sheer size is a mitigating factor. China is growing extremely fast (much faster than the U.S.) and has approximately 620 coal-fired power plants.[325] During the next four years, China is expected to add 160 new coal-fired power plants and India is expected to add 46 plants.[326] There appears to be an agreement from China regarding the reduction of carbon emissions. However, no specifics have been agreed upon and there is no current plan to monitor whether China complies.[327] Who is going to ensure that China complies? How is the U.S. going to obtain agreement from the governments of other countries to adopt new standards if these countries are experiencing economic difficulties and do not have the funds necessary to comply?

U.S. companies with operations in foreign countries, for the most part, operate under the U.S. environmental rules and thus are spreading these practices around the world. China, on the other hand, does not follow strict rules like the U.S. does and thus is spreading their practices not only in China, but wherever they operate around the world. It makes common sense that the focus should be on China first. However, common sense also dictates that you must be practical and focus on the places where there is a better chance of achieving success.

SUGGESTIONS:

1. Fund a research project to determine if anything other than nature has anything to do with our climate patterns. This project should have no outside funding or influencers with a political, economic, or environmental motive.
2. Continue to utilize the latest technology to update monitoring, analysis and process tools.

CHAPTER 19

THE GREAT POLITICAL DIVIDE

*Politics, it seems to me, for years, or all too long, has been concerned with right or left instead of right or wrong. – **Richard Armour**[328]*

Being a Democrat or a Republican comes with it a certain belief system. It also has an impact over who you listen to on the radio; who you choose to listen to in group discussions as well as where you choose to get your news on TV or the Internet. If you believe everything reported by the people you follow without researching it for yourself, you are being used.

Politicians and the media have learned from advertisers what sells and how to get people to believe in their way of thinking. Here is a tip. When a politician, journalist or TV personality elicits emotion over the facts to get their point across, they are trying to manipulate you. People are basically emotional and oftentimes fall for this tactic which is the reason why emotional advertising works.[329] People make decisions on emotion and then justify them with logic to make themselves feel as if they are making a rational decision.[330] Common sense dictates that both logic and emotion be utilized to make decisions not just emotion.

Whether you believe it or not, the Obama administration has had a polarizing effect on the country[331]. The left has gone further left in their thinking and the right has drifted further right in their thinking[332]. Why has this happened when the U.S. elected a President who was supposed to bring everyone together and provide the most transparent administration in history?[333] How can it be that the administration is doing something that they think will have a specific affect, but instead it has the reverse affect? This does not make common sense.

I believe the answer has to do with power and control as well as how and what the media reports. In addition, it has to do with how race is portrayed in America or at least how race is utilized to gain viewers or listeners. By utilizing dramatic headlines and cherry picking stories based on ideology, both sides have led the country into the big divide.[334] Furthermore, by continuing to misuse the word *racism*, I am sad to say that the term now has lost its meaning.[335] Was this the objective? Was the objective to divide? This is exactly what the results have indicated. Who wins if the country is more divided racially? Everyone loses.

The U.S. is more divided politically now than before we had an African American in the highest office. I did say politically. Americans have not changed their core beliefs just from watching and listening to the media, but it has the appearance that this has happened. This does not make common sense. By having an African American attaining the highest office, the country should have erased the racial divide and brought the country closer together. Instead many of the media outlets and some politicians continue to draw the race card be it African Americans, Asians, Hispanics, or others. [336]

Some of the media outlets cannot get past this divide and look upon all Americans as simply Americans.[337] The media utilizes race for dramatic effect to gain viewers and listeners. We live in a global world where races are virtually indistinguishable. There are intermarriages and relationships between ethnic and racial groups to where black and white are not black and white anymore. Why do some of the media outlets fail to recognize this?

Why has the Tea Party been portrayed in some media outlets as hateful while the 'Occupy Movement' which has utilized violence to get their point across has been given a pass and actually praised by some in the media?[338] Does a cause override the rule of law? This does not make common sense. Forget the message of each group and consider just the character and the way they present themselves. Which group acted more responsibly? Both groups deserve to be heard but only within the confines of the law. Law breakers should be dealt with swiftly no matter what the cause.

The U.S. is a country of laws and a country that promotes free speech whether the message corresponds with your beliefs or not. Why is free speech okay when the message agrees with the politics of the media outlets and termed hateful when it does not? Remember when the protestors against President George W. Bush were applauded by the media and those protesting against President Obama's policies were termed racists?[339] That does not make common sense when you consider journalists are supposed to report the news not editorialize it. Common sense dictates that both groups have a right to express their point of view but must adhere to the rule of law.

If the Occupy movement was called Occupy Tea Party movement, the rule of law would have been enforced from day one. What is fair is fair. This is one of the reasons why the U.S. has so many problems. The U.S. affords different groups preferential treatment just because of their message. You enjoy it when you are getting special treatment but resent it when somebody else with different beliefs is getting it. Common sense dictates that everyone is entitled to the same treatment no matter their beliefs.

The United States has historically been a centrist nation where the beliefs have been a combination of the left and the right's beliefs.[340] This has become increasingly difficult as the belief systems of both the left and the right have gone to the extremes. It is now an *either this or that* situation. There is middle ground on every issue but the climate seems to be a *whatever they want, we're against* situation. The U.S. must bring the left and right back to the center where they can actually work together and get things done. The U.S. is not an *either this or that* country but a *little of this and a little of that* country. Contact your representatives and let them know where their constituents stand.

SUGGESTIONS:

1. Contact your representatives and the media. Tell them the U.S. is made up of Americans: race is not a factor in everything that happens or everything that is done.
2. Remind your representatives the U.S. is a centrist nation and compromise is needed to get things done.
3. With the potentially life altering problems that are facing the U.S. today, ideology has no

place in the discussion. It is imperative that both sides come together.

4. The law is the law and should be enforced no matter what your beliefs.

5. Bring back truth in the news. Contact your media providers and tell them you want the facts and the truth not the providers spin.

CHAPTER 20

FRAUD AND ABUSE

"A decent and manly examination of the acts of government should be not only tolerated, but encouraged." **-- William Henry Harrison**[341]

The Federal Government is wrought with fraud and abuse and nobody seems to be doing much about it[342]. There is considerable talk from both political sides about how much fraud and abuse are costing the taxpayers. In fact, both sides have introduced plans that include savings from reducing fraud and abuse, but have not produced any specifics on how this will be accomplished. It is in vogue to use savings from fraud and abuse to fund new programs, but this argument is getting old and the American public will not be fooled for long. The cost to taxpayers is billions of dollars every year and continues to increase[343]. This money could be used to create jobs and get people off government assistance thus reducing the cost of government.

The Council of the Inspectors General on Integrity and Efficiency has the primary responsibility of detecting fraud, waste, abuse, and violations of law as well as promoting economy, efficiency, and effectiveness in the operations of the Federal Government[344]. While this organization has the responsibility of detecting fraud, waste, and abuse, they do not have the responsibility of correcting it or prosecuting individuals involved in the fraud and abuse. Is anything being done about this fraud, waste, and abuse?

When visiting the website of the Office of Inspector General (OIG), U.S. Department of Health & Human Services at oig.hhs.gov/fraud, the first item on the page is child support enforcement. Granted, the items appear to be in alphabetical order, nevertheless this does nothing to showcase their efforts to uncover fraud, waste, and abuse. Under the Reports & Publications tab, the fraud and abuse control program reports are listed by year which included the relevant information. In the 2013 Work Plan, there is mention of the Health Care Fraud Prevention and Enforcement Action Team (Heat) which was started in 2009 by the HHS and DOJ. Here is a direct quote in the report: "These teams, now a key component of HEAT, have a record of successfully analyzing data to quickly identify and prosecute fraud."[345] While HEAT is providing a much needed service, their mention of "quickly identify and prosecute" does not agree with the statistics.[346] I would expect that *quickly identify* to mean fraud of less than $10,000 not $1 million or higher. Common sense dictates that in order for fraud to be quickly identified, it should be detected well before the fraud exceeds $1 million.

Utilizing technology, a better way of cross-referencing organizations, tax returns, and individuals with Medicare/Medicaid/ACA expenditures is required if fraud and abuse is to be significantly reduced. In addition, the penalty for defrauding the Federal Government must be increased.

On the OIG U.S. Department of Health & Human Services Web site is a list of the most wanted fugitives who have been indicted or have had a felony complaint filed for Medicare/Medicaid fraud[347]. Each of these fugitives has defrauded the government of over $300,000 with the majority over $1 million and up to $40 million.[348] Why was the fraud not detected earlier? Are adequate controls and oversight in place to keep this from happening? Will the controls detect fraud before it elevates to these levels? Are effective controls in place so fraud will not extend to Obamacare?

The employees working in these government departments know much more about what is going on and where abuse and fraud might be found. A program should be developed that will offer incentives to federal employees for uncovering fraud and abuse. On the various U.S. government Web sites are instructions on how to report fraud and abuse but no mention of incentives or statistics on successful investigations utilizing Federal Government employee input. Each Federal Government department should participate in a program to uncover waste, fraud, and abuse offering monetary awards.

Common sense dictates that the Federal Government follow the private sector and hire independent auditors to audit every department. Security precautions would be required for those departments or areas that require a specific security clearance. This alone will save the taxpayers money and help balance the budget. One option is to utilize technology such as data mining to uncover patterns of abuse that could be investigated in a quicker manner. Another option is to elicit help of the large insurance companies on processes they utilize to combat fraud and abuse. It just makes common sense to utilize private sector policies to uncover fraud and abuse. In the private sector, companies would go out of business with the level of fraud and abuse that is rampant in the U.S. Federal Government. Common sense dictates a more prudent use of taxpayer money.

The penalties for defrauding the government are not sufficient enough to stop it or the laws are not being enforced. Common sense says that increasing the penalties for fraud should be invoked and investigated by a team consisting of the FBI and independent auditors to look into and combat fraud. Each area of the government should be prioritized in order of estimated dollar value of fraud and abuse and tackled in order from the highest to the lowest dollar amount.

Going forward, the team should investigate the departments on the list successively using the same tactics based on expected return. Once the fraud and abuse is under control in an area, safeguards should be installed to ensure that fraud and abuse does not return. In addition, the Attorney General's office must make it a priority to prosecute those apprehended. Once individuals and companies are held accountable, common sense indicates that a dramatic reduction in future fraud and abuse cases should occur.

Federal employees that are complicit in committing fraud or allowing abuse should be punished to the full extent of the law. They should be publically exposed so others will choose not to follow their lead.

Finally, the resultant fraud and abuse as well as the specific dollar amounts uncovered must be publicized for two reasons. The first reason is to let the taxpayers know that the Federal Government is actively working on increasing efficiency and reducing wasteful government spending on behalf of the American people. The second reason is to let those who are thinking of committing fraud against the government know that they will be prosecuted to the fullest extent of the law.

SUGGESTIONS:

1. Develop a program to provide incentives for federal employees to uncover fraud and abuse or lead investigators to where fraud and abuse might be taking place.
2. Hire independent consultants to audit all departments utilizing technology such as data mining tools to uncover abuse and waste.
3. Estimate the level of fraud and abuse by department based on an estimated dollar value.
4. Tackle the estimated fraud and abuse in order of estimated return.
5. Elicit the FBI to work in conjunction with the independent auditors to investigate and uncover cases of fraud.
6. Increase the penalties for fraud.
7. Actively prosecute individuals and companies for perpetrating fraud.

CHAPTER 21

GOVERNMENT PAY AND PENSIONS

"The government is merely a servant -- merely a temporary servant; it cannot be its prerogative to determine what is right and what is wrong, and decide who is a patriot and who isn't. Its function is to obey orders, not originate them."
— Mark Twain[349]

Companies in the private sector must compete or go out of business. This is simple and straightforward.

In order to compete, companies continually scrutinize employee salaries, benefits and pension packages.

In the private sector, large corporations hire consulting firms to conduct annual surveys of salary and benefit packages for all positions or levels within the company.[350] Based on the survey results, companies can ascertain whether their pay and benefit package offerings are consistent with the offerings of other companies in the same or similar industries.

There have been several studies by partisan groups on the differences between pay and benefit packages for companies in the private sector versus those in the public sector.[351] However, none of the studies have come up with definitive or conclusive findings.[352] The Congressional Budget Office (CBO) compiled a report at the behest of the ranking member of the Senate Budget Committee.[353] While the results of this study indicated Federal workers on average received higher wages and benefits, the differences were reversed when contrasting those with a professional degree or doctorate.[354]

The fairest way to resolve this issue on whether government pay and benefits are competitive is to hire an outside consultant familiar with performing salary and benefit surveys. The consultant should develop a methodology to compare jobs within the government just like the private sector. Benefit packages should also be compared as Federal Government employees receive benefits greater than the private sector.[355]

This new comparison methodology should be instituted on an annual basis to ensure consistency.

In the private sector, employees are fired when they do not perform based on predetermined standards. When employees do not adhere to strict company policies regarding instances of sexual harassment or other egregious acts that shine a bad light on the company or the company image, there are consequences that include demotion or dismissal.

While you can fire employees in the public sector, it is very difficult to do.[356] The best way to fire a federal employee is to downsize their department. Even then factors such as personal performance, type of employment (career, appointee or probationary), length of service, veteran's preference rights, and performance rating must be considered.[357] Subsequently, the employee has a chance to fix their performance problems and appeal the decision. The aforementioned increases the timeframe in which to rid a department of an ineffective employee and makes the entire process quite costly.[358] In the end, it is easier to re-assign the employee then to go through the hoops of firing them. This would not happen in the private sector as companies cannot afford to retain people who are not productive. Why should public sector employees be treated differently than private sector employees? Common sense says to change the policy. Mimic that of the private sector which results in better performance from the employees, increases efficiency and reduces costs to the taxpayer.

FEDERAL GOVERNMENT PENSIONS

One concession made by the majority of companies in the private sector was to eliminate company pensions and switch to employee funded 401ks with matching company contributions. Switching to a 401k plan puts the onus on the employee to manage and fund their retirement. While the government has a Thrift Savings Plan (TSP) similar to the private sector 401k plan, the primary retirement plan is still a defined benefits pension plan which results in a disconnect between the public and private sectors. As a matter of fact, in 2011 unfunded Federal Government pension obligations increased over 20% from 2010 and are on pace to double in the next 10 years.[359]

In fiscal year 2011, the federal unfunded pension liability topped at $761.5 billion which is $139 billion more than the prior year.[360] The current Federal Employee Retirement system (FERS) was created in the early 1980's to replace the Civil Service Retirement and Disability Fund (CSRDF) which has never been fully funded.[361] As the U.S. population ages so does the roll of pension recipients and the yearly expense. President Obama endorsed a proposal to increase the pension participation by the federal employees. While this will definitely help, it will not slow the increase in unfunded pension liabilities enough to make a real difference.

What is required to reverse the trend is to eliminate the government pension systems (FERS and CSRDF) and move toward a sole 401k system like the private sector. To begin the transition, the new 401k system or TSP, should only apply to new government hires and these new hires will not participate in the Federal Employee Retirement system (FERS). However, this step alone will not be enough. To completely reverse the trend, the entire FERS should be abandoned and replaced with TSP. The commitment to those who have already retired or are close to retirement must be honored. The U.S. has reached a point where it must enact solutions to problems that would not ordinarily be solutions of choice.

It is important the transition be made for federal employees as soon as possible as this will hopefully have a cascading effect on state and local public employees. I believe state and local municipalities will see the light and follow suit. The underlying reasons why states have not made the transition already are twofold. First, the change is so dramatic that it will be political suicide for the politician who recommends it. Second, states follow the Federal Government's lead. The states are waiting for the Federal Government to make the transition which will give them a tangible reason to follow suit and lessen the political fallout.

California realized their problem and instituted pension reform by raising employee contributions and increasing the retirement age of public employees.[362] In fact, from 2009 to 2011, there were 43 states that enacted some type of pension reform.[363] Although pension changes have been enacted and the states should be applauded for their efforts, the best way to institute lasting pension reform and reduce the unfunded liabilities is to move away from defined pension plans to a 401k type plan.

By making the transition to a 401k type plan, the growing unfunded pension liabilities will be curbed. As in Detroit, unfunded pension liabilities are in epidemic proportions throughout the country. For example, the city of Chicago has an unfunded pension liability of over $19 billion and the outlook only gets bleaker in the future. New York is another city with billions of unfunded pension liability. In total, all state and municipal government pensions are estimated to be under funded by $730 billion to $4.4 trillion depending on the rate used to discount future pension obligations.[364] To use a medical analogy, if the bleeding is not stopped, the patient will die. This solution does not address the unfunded healthcare liability which is an entirely different, but very important, matter.

Taking into account the increasing size of the Federal Government, the growing number and size of pensions, and reduced number of workers in the workforce, the results are an untenable, unsustainable situation. Common sense dictates that the Federal Government should do away with traditional pensions and substitute 401k plans with matching provisions. Start the transition with new hires and then move on to workers age 40 or less so those close to retirement or those who have already retired will not be affected. If the U.S. does not make the changes soon, it will be too late and the affects will be irreversible.

SUGGESTIONS:

1. Change the policy on firing employees to more closely resemble that of the private sector.
2. Conduct an external salary and benefits survey and adjust packages accordingly.
3. Transition from the Federal Employee Retirement system (FERS) to a 401k system starting with new hires and then extending to those workers who are 40 and under.
4. Encourage state and local governments to follow the lead of the federal government in transitioning to a 401k plan.

CHAPTER 22

STUDENT LOAN PROGRAM

"A student loan is like any other loan, it must be paid back. Tread carefully and don't take on more than you can handle." **– Dan Craddock**

Students view student loans merely as a means to obtain a college education. Their focus is on the short-term to solve a lack of funds problem. Students are not interested in rationalizing the total funds borrowed with the yearly income expected from a chosen profession coupled with the expense of a monthly loan payback. Relatively cheap, readily available funds are very enticing to a student with a single short-term focus of obtaining a college education. Rarely do students consider the long-term ramifications of these student loans which, is the real problem.

Of the nearly 21 million Americans who attend college each year, approximately 12 million or 60% take out student loans to help fund their college education.[365] Since 2007, student loans have doubled to an estimated $1.2 trillion. [366] The second largest form of household debt in the nation is now student loan debt. Student loans surpass all other forms of debt except mortgages. The average balance on a student loan is now $26,000.[367] Five or ten years after college, student loan debt is causing young adults to avoid buying cars and homes which has a ripple effect on the economy.[368] In addition, student loan debt is causing young workers to either reduce or not contribute to a 401k plan which has a detrimental long-term effect on their retirement plans.[369]

The government took over the student loan program in 2010.[370] The reason given was that the government could administer the program cheaper than banks by not having to pay the banks a subsidy. In addition, the surplus savings would be utilized for Pell Grants for needy students, community colleges and minority-serving colleges. There have been no savings and above that, the government cut the interest rate in half to 3.4%. Can you recall any program that the government has taken over that has not cost more than it did in the private sector?

What makes common sense is to have interest rates increase as inflation increases just like mortgage rates. Moreover, the interest rate at the time of approval would be fixed for the life of the student loan. For example, a loan for each year of school would most likely carry a different interest rate. This is fair and will keep the program solvent.

As a matter of fact, this concept was signed into law by President Obama.[371] Student loans should not have risen to 6.8% considering how low interest rates are currently. With the new higher rates, the government stands to make billions which hopefully can be utilized to pay down the national debt.[372]

More than 33 million workers may qualify for student loan forgiveness, but the government red tape is so complicated that few take advantage of the benefit.[373] Common sense says to simplify the process so those who are eligible can take advantage of it. Common sense also says to extend the eligibility for student loan forgiveness to Doctors as they will be in short supply due to Obamacare.[374]

Besides the mounting outstanding student loan debt, one of the biggest issues is the rising cost of a college education. The increased cost of education has a direct effect on the increasing student loan debt. Over the last 30 years, college tuition has increased over 1,000%.[375] To put this into perspective, rising healthcare costs and housing costs have not increased as much as tuition costs.[376] This is an incredible phenomenon. Although there has been some talk about it, there has been no tangible effort to reduce the cost of higher education. Do you know of any college that has instituted a program to reduce the cost of tuition? Is the quality of education better now than it was 10 or 20 years ago? Why have costs gone up so much when competition keeps increasing? This is counter intuitive and not indicative of the free market system.

Many private colleges and universities have embarked on cost-cutting programs to lower payroll costs, lower energy costs, and institute wellness programs.[377] However, these programs are meant to stem rising operating and administrative costs not to reduce costs to students. While these cost-saving measures may slow the increase in costs, students will not see any immediate impact.

Colleges are essentially taking advantage of students because students have ready access to cheap money. Controls have been instituted on credit card companies to limit the issuance to those individuals who are under the age of 21 to keep these companies from preying on young students.[378] However, there have been no such reforms on student loans.

Logically, with all of the online schools cropping up, tuition costs should go down since competition reduces costs. Remember learning about supply and demand? Well, tuition costs keep going up so there must be a reason for it. The reason is cheap, readily available student loan money and the fact that the private sector is competing with the public sector. Since money is readily available for students, there is no incentive for schools to reduce tuition costs. The schools know the money is there and most schools will actively assist the student in obtaining a student loan. Only when money is tight and enrollment drops off will schools feel the pressure and begin to reduce tuition costs. Common sense dictates that state schools should take the lead and initiate an external audit of costs and expenditures with the result being a reduction in tuition costs. Once state schools reduce tuition costs, private institutions will follow suit.

There is a definite lack of education concerning the overall cost of a student loan and the long-term effect associated with assuming said student loan debt. While each recipient signs an agreement which indicates the monthly payment amounts and the total number of years required to pay off the loan, this is not sufficient. Each recipient should also be supplied with a chart detailing the expected income of each profession so the student can estimate whether they can expect an income sufficient enough to afford the monthly loan payments along with their other monthly obligations. More education upfront will provide potential loan recipients with the needed information and cut down on over borrowing.

Depending on the particular chosen profession, attending a private university for four years might not be the best option. The better option might be to attend an online or state school requiring a smaller student loan. This would provide a better assurance that the loan would be paid back and the student would not be financially strapped.

In addition, potential student loan recipients should be presented with an additional strategy that involves attending a community college or online school in the first two years and then transferring to a major school for the remaining two years. Both of these options would result in a significant reduction in student loan debt for the recipient and might be the best strategy when considering the long-term effects.

Before the government took over the student loan program, there were a large percentage of student loan defaults. A stronger message should be lauded from the inception of the loan that the student loan must be paid back. As was stated, there are student loan forgiveness programs, but they are complex and most people decline to take advantage of them. Now that the IRS is the enforcer for delinquent student loan debt, this fact should be prominently displayed on the loan in large, bold letters and conveyed in strong terms to the recipient. If history is any indication, students deciding to default on student loan debt will experience many problems.[379]

SUGGESTIONS:

1. Simplify the student loan forgiveness process.
2. Extend the student loan forgiveness program to include doctors who will be in short supply due to Obamacare.
3. State schools should institute external audits of their costs with the emphasis on lowering tuition costs.
4. Pressure should be put on private institutions to bring down tuition costs.
5. More education should be provided to students on the effects of obtaining a student loan.
6. Student loan applications should include a schedule of different professions along with the expected annual pay.
7. Education on loan repayment as well as loan repayment enforcement by the IRS should be provided.
8. Potential student loan recipients should be given alternatives like attending a community college or online school for either two or four years to reduce potential future debt.

CHAPTER 23

NATIONAL DEFENSE

"There is a rank due to the United States, among nations, which will be withheld, if not absolutely lost, by the reputation of weakness. If we desire to avoid insult, we must be able to repel it; if we desire to secure peace, one of the most powerful instruments of our rising prosperity; it must be known that we are at all times ready for war." **- George Washington**[380]

Whether or not this opinion is well-liked, the U.S. is the most powerful nation on earth and has a responsibility to keep the peace. If not the U.S., then who? In order to do this, the U.S. must have a defense department that is second to none and is up-to-date with the newest, ever-changing technology. This means the U.S. must address the very serious cyber-threats as well as continue to increase the capabilities of the armed forces.

By utilizing up-to-date technology as well as drones, the U.S. reduces its armed forces personnel resulting in a more efficient and effective military.[381] Technology has saved many soldiers' lives and will continue to save more lives. However, vigilance and investment in the military must continue. Yes, invest which means to spend more money. This is one area that an increase in spending is warranted although it will be offset somewhat in a reduction of military personnel. By utilizing the latest technology, continuously upgrading ships, aircraft, and weaponry, the U.S. will retain its strong military presence.

Education is the key to having a technologically advanced national defense. President Obama has the right idea by promoting education in the science, technology, engineering and math (STEM) disciplines.[382] A concerted program sponsored by the Federal Government with participation from the business community will provide students with the information they need to pursue one of these paths.

The program should promote and demonstrate the use of STEM disciplines.

The U.S. STEM Education Model developed by the Raytheon Company tracks students from kindergarten through grade 16 and into business and teaching professions in the STEM disciplines.[383] This model as well as increased coordination between business and education will help the U.S. create the workforce required to compete in the global economy.

A better way to recruit the best minds to work for the U.S. government is sorely needed. The issue of money and perks from companies in the video game industry and other lucrative businesses must be addressed or the most-technologically minded individuals will be lost to private industry. Common sense dictates that special pay grades with retention bonuses for highly intelligent and skilled people should be established. However, the main incentive should be patriotism not money.

Patriotism is a part of America's history and is the reason the U.S. is a free nation. Patriots through the years have risen up to accept the challenge and ensure that the country remains free. The U.S. owes a great debt of gratitude to its veterans and those who have performed their patriotic duty serving the country. It is every American's duty to serve the country be it in the military, politics, or some other way in order to continue the traditions held so dear. The freedoms afforded U.S. citizens are something that cannot be taken for granted lest they be taken away.

President Obama has taken the drone program to a new level which has proven to be very effective in the fight against terrorism.[384] Further advances in this program as well as other areas of the military will continue to be required. Ensuring the safety of the U.S. and the men and women in the armed forces is the military's highest priority. By enhancing the drone programs in the air, on land, on the sea, and under the sea, the U.S. can maintain its role as the world's peace keeper.

Using a sports analogy, a good defense wins ballgames (I believe the Seattle Seahawks would agree). By strengthening military capabilities for defensive as well as offense purposes will serve as a deterrent to those who want to harm the U.S. and their way of life. If the U.S. does not continue to enhance its military capabilities and maintain defensive bases around the world, they will be subject to the whims of other countries that do not like the American way of life and want to destroy it.

If the U.S. is to defeat terrorism then the first step is to call it what it is and not soften or distort its nature. Terrorists are terrorists foreign or domestic whether they are acting based on religious beliefs or some distorted reasons. Their sole purpose is to kill pure and simple, whether their targets are infidels, military personnel, executives, government workers, or their own co-workers. Americans need to stand together and defeat all terrorism by keeping their eyes and ears open to possible threats to the country and its people.

It would be a lofty goal to have terrorism eradicated, but in reality the U.S. can make great strides to put a dent in it.

SUGGESTIONS:

1. Continue to increase the technological capabilities of the armed forces.
2. Reduce military manpower in favor of technology.
3. Utilize drones in the air, on land, on sea, and under the sea to keep the nation safe.
4. Develop a pay structure and retention system to recruit and retain highly intelligent minds.
5. Develop a program sponsored by the Federal Government in conjunction with the business community to promote and demonstrate real world applications of the STEM disciplines. The end result being an increase in scientific, technological, engineering, and mathematical professionals.
6. Be up front with the American people about terrorism and call it what it is.
7. Assist efforts to confront terrorism by keeping your eyes and ears open and reporting unusual activities to the proper authorities.

CHAPTER 24

HEALTHCARE REFORM

"People spending more of their own money on routine health care would make the system more competitive and transparent and restore the confidence between the patients and the doctors without government rationing". – **Dr. Benjamin Carson**[385]

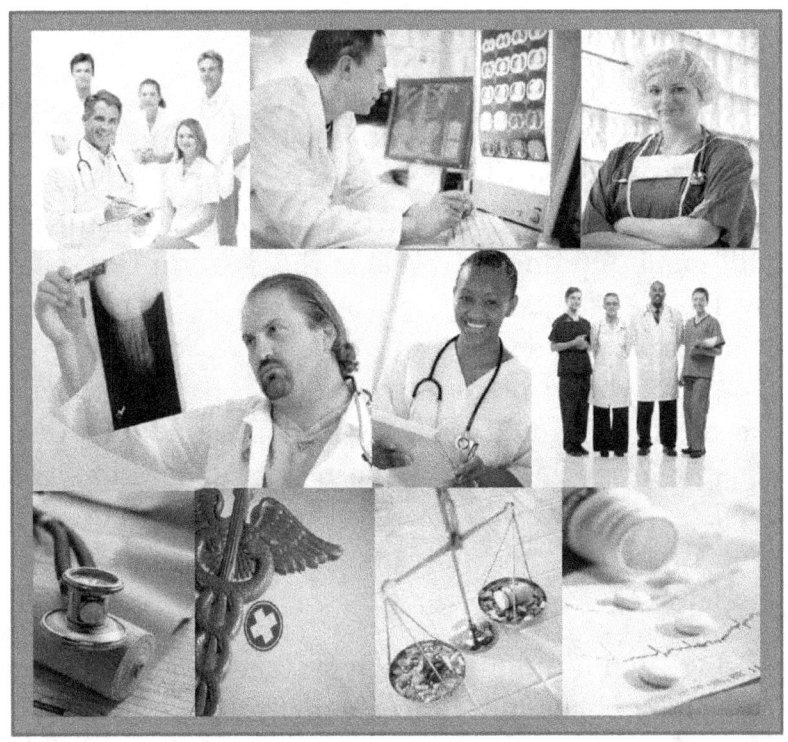

Whether you call it the Affordable Care Act (ACA), Obamacare, Healthcare Reform, or Universal

Healthcare, this system will forever change the lives of all Americans. The sheer size of the undertaking is mind boggling. Just imagine what it would take to set up a healthcare system that will service tens of millions of people basically from scratch. That is what has to happen with the new healthcare system. The cost of setting up exchanges for all 50 states, setting up training programs on how to use the exchanges, and developing Internet sites with the proper, required, security protocols is in the billions of dollars. No wonder the writers of this law incorporated so many new taxes in the legislation that will affect all Americans.

The role out of the Affordable Care Act website has been less than stellar. In fact, it has been a disaster.[386] Costs for building the website have skyrocketed and the system is riddled with problems requiring additional funding.[387] When the government gets involved, costs tend to go up. To top it off, the contract to build the website went to a Canadian company who also has many other U.S. government contracts. Granted, this Canadian company, CGI Federal, has a United States arm but the question still persists: Why wasn't an American company chosen? Are American technology companies not good enough?

Having been a programmer, a systems analyst, and a Project Manager developing a multitude of systems both domestic and international, I possess a reasonable knowledge of what is required in a system of this magnitude. Once the software has been written and the individual modules have been tested, the next steps are a full end-to-end system test and then user testing. User testing encompasses a series of rigorous testing of every facet of the system starting with a predetermined set of data and known outcomes. Another component of user testing is simulating the expected traffic on the website. The objective of all this testing is to ensure the system performs to specifications. Any problems encountered during the testing are logged and fixed and another round of testing is done. The system is not signed off as completed until all problems have been resolved and the appropriate response times are met on a consistent basis. Apparently this step in the process was missed.

In addition, a system of this type should have security built-in from day one to protect sensitive information from hackers. This is another area that has been riddled with problems.[388]

The success of Obamacare hinges on getting younger Americans to sign up for healthcare.[389] Being that younger Americans are so familiar with technology, the persistent problems with the Obamacare website has hindered enrollment. Most of the State exchanges, on the other hand, are not having the same problems as the federal Web site and enrollment appears to be progressing albeit slower than expected.[390]

Health premiums as well as deductibles in most states are going up and in some cases quite significantly.[391] The increases are dependent upon the particular state a person resides in and their age. Furthermore, premium increases were not part of the initial plan and are reported to be over 20% in some states.[392]

Where is the U.S. going to get the doctors to service the millions and millions of new healthcare recipients?[393] Does the new healthcare law address this or address the cost of educating all these new doctors that will be required? No. Common sense says to deal with the shortage of doctors before passing a bill that will add millions of patients to the system. Since the U.S. government did not address the lack of doctors before passing the bill, it makes common sense that it be addressed after passing the bill. This issue has not yet been mentioned. According to the Association of American Medical Colleges, there is currently a shortage of 13,000 doctors.[394] With the addition of 30 million people to the insurance rolls, the doctor shortage is expected to increase ten-fold within the next 12 years to 130,000.[395]

Of the existing doctors, more and more of them are not taking on new Obamacare patients or are opting to retire.[396] In addition, concierge medicine catering to the wealthy is also taking doctors away from the masses.[397] How will this affect the doctor shortage?

An alternative to the doctor shortage is to recruit foreign doctors and streamline the entry process.[398]

Other countries are experiencing doctor shortages as well and are actively taking steps to recruit and train foreign doctors.[399] We will be behind the curve and must now rev up efforts to compete with these countries for medical resources. Even if we are successful in enticing foreign doctors to work in the U.S., lowering our standards will jeopardize the level of patient care that we expect from our physicians. Improperly trained physicians can potentially lead to wrong diagnoses, non-diagnoses, and increased deaths.

One way to alleviate some of the doctor shortage is by offering incentives. For instance, the U.S. could reduce or subsidize the cost of medical school for American students in exchange for a promise to practice medicine in the U.S. for a set number of years. However, we must be mindful of the added cost of providing this benefit. Since the cost of healthcare is already rising too quickly, a concerted plan to lower the cost while still providing the needed financial benefits to potential doctors must be prepared before implementation can realistically occur. Ideally, this plan should have been implemented prior to the passing of the bill.

The initial estimate of the cost of universal healthcare was around $940 billion for the first ten years.[400] It has not even been fully implemented and cost estimates from the Congressional Budget Office (CBO) have gone up to over $1.8 trillion.[401] This is an extra burden for the American taxpayer over and above the huge national debt and there is no way of knowing how high the costs will go.

It is no secret that the U.S. healthcare system needed to be reformed. However, no one could have imagined a change of this magnitude was envisioned. In fact, the majority of Americans believe the ACA should either be revised or eliminated.[402] Only time will tell whether the ACA was a good idea, but if cost is the gauge, then it is not looking good.

Universal healthcare was passed by Congress on a partisan basis and was done rapidly while the Democrats had a majority in both the Senate and House of Representatives. It was done so quickly that Congress was not given the time to read the bill before they voted on it. Common sense dictates that any law should be thoroughly read and discussed prior to being put up for a vote. The bill itself was over 2,200 pages and regulations coming from this bill span more than 10,500 pages and counting.[403] To put this into perspective, the Medicare Modernization Act of 2003 yielded about 5,000 pages of regulations in the first three years after being passed.[404] Can implementation problems be expected?

There are individuals who say if the Affordable Care Act was not passed in this manner that it would never have been passed.[405] Congress has already voted down some of the new tax provisions that were part of the original bill. Common sense says if Congress had read the bill before voting on it, the bill would not have needed revisions prior to implementation. What else is Congress going to retract or revise? Certain provisions, like the employer mandate for companies with over 50 employees are being delayed, so what else can be expected?

Union management, who supported the Affordable Care Act and actively campaigned for its passage, has now realized that many union members may be adversely affected.[406] In hindsight, they want to keep their current healthcare plan much like most people who currently have healthcare coverage. Also, union members are afraid the healthcare act might cause their full-time employment status to turn into part-time status due to the 30-hour week mandate in Obamacare.[407]

Most people are in agreement that healthcare reform was badly needed. However, universal agreement was not met on exactly how to do it, what it would look like, or whether it would be a federal or state issue. It is now evident that some of the initial promises cannot be kept, like being able to keep your current insurance. It is not readily apparent what other issues will come to light in the future. If history is any indication when government gets involved the costs rise significantly.

Employer-offered healthcare was doomed from the start especially due to the limited options for self-employed or unemployed workers. It does not seem fair that the cost of healthcare is based on where a person works. The largest companies offer the lowest priced insurance because of the huge buying power they represent. You could sit in a doctor's office next to another patient who is paying twice as much for the same insurance coverage only because you work for different companies. At a minimum, state-sponsored insurance exchanges should have been offered as a challenge to the large employers so everyone received an equal amount of insurance at a reasonable rate.

Additionally, tort reform and the ability to purchase insurance across state lines should have been addressed. Caps on legal judgments against medical practitioners should have been passed to reduce the required amount of medical malpractice insurance a doctor must carry thus lowering the cost of healthcare. Common sense says that a major portion of this reduction should be passed on to consumers. Purchasing insurance across state lines will increase competition which should reduce costs. Both of these provisions should have been included in the healthcare reform and would have reduced costs. The former would have increased the incentive for Americans to enter medical school.

Why was the full time workweek definition changed to 30 hours in the Obamacare law? It appears that this provision has had the opposite effect. Instead of employers providing insurance to more employees, employers are reducing hours of employees to fewer than 30 so they do not have to offer insurance to them. Common sense says to revise the law and change the full time worker hours back to 40.

Universally, we probably all want efficient healthcare that does not exclude us for pre-existing conditions and contains at least the same level of coverage that most people who are currently insured enjoy. As we get older, we tend to rely more and more on our personal physician and value their advice. With Obamacare, our doctor will still be in charge but only up to a point. The Independent Payment Advisory Board (IPAB) established in ACA is responsible for controlling healthcare costs.[408] In a study of head and neck surgeons, 27% believe the ACA creates death panels.[409] Doctors might not have a choice on certain treatments due to a generalized policy on cost reduction.

Currently, major treatment decisions are made by insurance companies guided by recommendations from your doctor. Hence, if there is a disagreement with the Insurance company decision, an insurer can consult the insurance company's dispute policy. It remains to be seen where the insurance companies fit in and whether decisions by the IPAB in Washington are disputable.

How will the new healthcare law affect the average person who currently has insurance through their employer or through an outside vendor? Firstly, their current insurance may be in jeopardy. Many employers have already decided to cancel employee coverage and pay the fine rather than continue to offer insurance. This decision was primarily based on economics. Secondly, retirees who receive health insurance from their former employer may experience a break in coverage. Companies must compete both domestically and globally. Therefore, if one company in an industry decides to cancel retiree coverage, then others will likely follow suit. It is pure economics.

As of November 14, 2013, there have been 27 significant changes made to Obamacare since the law was originally passed.[410] Of these 27 changes, 15 were made by Congress, 2 by the Supreme Court and 10 by President Obama.[411] Since the law is not fully implemented yet, there will probably be countless more changes. With this in mind, common sense says that the law should have been read and understood before the law was passed.

As far as patient care, there are several areas where patients might experience delays:

- in obtaining appointments,
- in obtaining approvals for additional tests or surgeries,
- in surgeries,
- in getting certain medications, and
- in obtaining physical therapy.

The delays mentioned above may or may not affect you. Changes can be dependent upon where a person lives. Therefore, if your area has limited changes, you may not be affected at all. However, in some locations, there will be massive changes including an increase in premiums as well as delays in obtaining healthcare services.

In actuality, it is unclear as to what Americans can expect from this new law because everyone's situation is different. The fact that the Internal Revenue Service (IRS) will have access to our private medical information and play the role of 'enforcer' is scary enough.[412] No one wants to hear from the IRS and now it appears as if the agency will have a greater presence in the lives of Americans.

The established exchanges will have access to your social security number as well as your medical information. The rise in identity theft and a greater accessibility to one's personal information creates a greater chance for an identity to be stolen.

The IRS will be adding over 1,000 employees to administer healthcare compliance.[413] Many people in America are not required to file a tax return because they fall outside of the tax filing guidelines established by the IRS.[414] Will this change due to Obamacare? There has been no policy issued at the time of this writing about the 2014 income tax reporting guidelines.

Here is what is known. The IRS is in charge of compliance and as such will need information from every U.S. citizen indicating whether they have insurance, are entitled to a government subsidy, or must pay a fine.[415] This can be done by creating a separate reporting apparatus. However, if current reporting is based on the various types of 1040 forms, then it only makes common sense to continue utilizing the same form with the newly incorporated information. Any option will mean additional work for the IRS and tax professionals with increased cost to the taxpayer. What about those individuals who have not filed a tax return over the years but should have? Is it time to totally revamp the tax system?

Now that the government is in charge of healthcare, it is no longer humanitarian; it is economics that guides the decisions. The government has no Hippocratic Oath to uphold.

If you are young you presumably have a long productive life remaining, and therefore will be given the best possible care available. On the other hand, if you are elderly, you might not receive an expensive procedure recommended by your doctor and instead be given medication. Is this true? I hope not especially because I am one of many who are getting up there in age. The whole system hinges on reducing costs. In 2009, Sarah Palin publicized the Death Panels that have since been debunked by many. However, the regulations are still evolving so the future is unclear at the present time. What is known is that the sole function of the IPAB is to cut healthcare costs.

No one wants to hear about a reduction in care for a loved one but how else can costs be reduced? Since the government will be overseeing the healthcare processes and cost-reduction strategies, common sense indicates that the logical way to reduce costs is to reduce the number of allowable procedures, eliminate second opinions and prescribe more medication.[416] What do you think?

There is an alternative to the Affordable Care Act, but the alternative is too expensive for the average American. Wealthy individuals will choose to go outside the system, obtain their own premium, and pay for a Cadillac healthcare plan. This is what happens in other countries that have universal healthcare. The rich will not have to wait for procedures. They will not have to wait for doctors. Doctors will be jumping at the chance to administer medicine to the rich. It will be the poor and the middle class who have to live within the confines of the new law.

Harry Reid, the Senate Majority Leader, said in an August 9, 2013 appearance on the Vegas PBS program *Nevada Week in Review*: "What we've done with Obamacare is have a step in the right direction, but we're far from having something that's going to work forever."[417] When asked if the country would have to abandon insurance as a means of accessing it, Reid said: "Yes, yes. Absolutely, yes."[418]

Obamacare is an interim system utilized to transition Americans to a government run single payer system. Is this the way ACA was sold to the American public? Is this what Americans want? What about the promise that individuals could keep their current health insurance?

Common sense says beware of politicians who tell you whatever you want to hear to get a bill passed in Congress. Americans should have taken heed when Nancy Pelosi said "we have to pass the bill so that you can find out what is in it...."[419] There is not much common sense in that statement, no matter which side of the aisle you sit on.

SUGGESTIONS:

1. Delay the implementation of Obamacare until all of the provisions can be worked out by both parties.
2. Add tort reform to the law.
3. Add the ability to purchase insurance across state lines to the law.
4. Include all federal employees as participants in ACA.
5. Reduce subsidies to Congress for health insurance since others at their income level are not afforded any subsidies.
6. Provide incentives and cost reductions for students who wish to enter medical school.
7. Reduce residency requirement and recruit more foreign doctors to fill the needed vacancies.
8. Prepare a rigorous plan to lower rising costs of healthcare without jeopardizing patient care.
9. Communicate with local representatives about not wanting a single payer, government run healthcare system.

CHAPTER 25

CONCLUSION

"Common sense is the most widely shared commodity in the world, for every man is convinced that he is well supplied with it." **— René Descartes**[420]

It cannot be stated enough that more common sense in government is needed. Ideology and partisanship has no place in the equation while the U.S. is facing such dramatic and explosive problems. A responsive, cohesive government willing to tackle the difficult issues is sorely needed now, while there is still a chance. No more kicking the proverbial can down the road. The problems will only get worse by ignoring them and possible solutions narrow as time goes by. Many people experience this in their daily lives as they try to pay bills, look for work, educate their children, etc. In my experience, a small unresolved problem can quickly become a huge problem if left unaddressed. Common sense dictates that business as usual is not an option. Issues should not focus on whether political points can be gained, but rather on the welfare of the American people.

The parallels with the downfall of ancient Rome to what is happening within our government are uncanny.[421] The Roman Empire was wrought with decay as the government became too big to control. Decadence and lavish, loose lifestyles, corrupt, and incompetent officials all led to the decline of the Roman Empire.[422]

Today government agencies like the IRS are spending enormous amounts of money for parties, creating unnecessary videos, having lavish conferences and participating in partisan politics.[423] Scandals regarding the investigation of journalists to Benghazi are being uncovered.[424] Out of control spending, increased dependency on government, loose morals, widespread fraud and abuse, and increased violence from groups like the Occupy movement are some of the reasons the U.S. is heading in the wrong direction. In ancient Rome, the emperor continued to conquer in order to fund ever-increasing government and lavish lifestyle. Today, the U.S. dollar continues to be devalued with the non-stop printing of money needed to fund an ever-increasing government, a mounting national debt, and growing dependency on government.[425] With the passing of the Affordable Care Act, the U.S. has now transitioned almost one sixth of the economy from the private sector to the Federal Government.[426]

At the end of this book is a list of *my wants*. Hopefully this book has inspired and motivated you to create your own list of wants and convey them to your elected representatives. It is the patriotic duty of all Americans to make America the safest, fairest, most innovative, most caring, and most opportunity-filled place on earth to live, work, and play. This should apply to you, your children, grandchildren, etc. The momentum is there so let your voice be heard. May God Bless America!

In conclusion, I will end with a dynamic quote by Thomas Paine: *"I love the man that can smile in trouble, that can gather strength from distress, and grow brave by reflection. 'Tis the business of little minds to shrink; but he whose heart is firm, and whose conscience approves his conduct, will pursue his principles unto death."*[427]

MY WANTS

I want the U.S. to succeed and prosper.

I want all Americans to have an equal opportunity to succeed.

I want the government to promote tax paying jobs in the private sector.

I want the government to promote and encourage entrepreneurship.

I want the government to adhere to our constitution and the principles therein.

I want government fraud and abuse to be stopped and the guilty to be prosecuted to the fullest extent of the law.

I want the Pledge of Allegiance to be recited in all schools.

I want people who do not like our country or our freedoms to leave or not be allowed to enter the U.S.

I want a strong, proud national defense to serve as a deterrent, not an offensive weapon.

I want terrorists to be called terrorists no matter what religion or from what country they hail.

I want Freedom of Religion to be embraced not just tolerated.

I want those showing their faith to be applauded not persecuted for it.

I want the principles of morality and ethics to be the cornerstones of the American way of life.

I want American businesses to be able to compete with foreign businesses by lowering corporate tax rates and reducing regulations.

I want corporate CEO's and upper management to be held accountable and suffer the consequences when the business falters.

I want American workers to compete with and surpass foreign workers.

I want our borders to be secure and, once secure, I want illegal immigrants to either be sent back to their home country or given the opportunity to gain citizenship. I want to be realistic so sending illegal immigrants home is really not an option given the extent of the problem.

I want foreign workers who work here for ten years or more, collect social security, then move back to their home country to receive reduced benefits based on their home countries cost of living or not at all.

I want the national language of the United States to be English. I want it to be a requirement that all signs be written in English and mandatory for all immigrants to learn English before becoming an American citizen.

I want our history to be relished and embraced not discounted or re-written.

I want our country to be unique and admired.

I want education to stress science, innovation, and technology.

I want equal pay for men and women.

I want all people to have healthcare but it should not be based on one's employment.

I want choices for my healthcare and do not want the government involved in the choice.

I want true reform of healthcare.

I want to outlaw lobbyists of any kind.

I want to reduce the number of lawyers and lawsuits.

I want a handshake to mean something.

I want welfare to be reformed and those who can work to work for their check.

I want Americans to work together in a bipartisan way for the good of the country.

I want to pay down our national debt so our children and grandchildren are not burdened with our debts.

I want term limits for Congress.

I want children to be able to play in the streets without fear of being abducted or abused.

I want discipline to start in the home and bring back spankings. (Lord knows I had my share)

I want parents, schools and businesses to work together to ensure that our children receive a quality education.

I want children left behind who will not take responsibility for their own education.

I want our schools to be the best in the world.

I want our teachers to receive better pay and benefits along with the accountability and consequences that accompany it.

I want fast food chains to increase the price of the unhealthiest foods and lower prices of the healthy food items.

I want grocery stores to lower the prices on healthy foods and increase prices on unhealthy foods.

I want mandatory physical education classes in school and mandatory physical tests in order to graduate.

I want American companies to be held accountable for their long-term strategies and short-term shortfalls.

I want employee bonuses to be given for long-term performance not short-term success.

I want unions to become extinct because they are not needed or wanted.

I want racism to be a thing of the past and not an issue that confronts us every day.

I want us not to need organizations that advance a certain race or ethnicity.

I want competitions and awards given to those deserving of them.

I want people to be motivated to do their best and be proud of their accomplishments.

I want to get back the America of which I am so proud.

~ ~

COMMON SENSE GUIDES

This is the second in a series of Common Sense Books designed to provide you with sound and practical advice. Be on the lookout for future Books.

See also
"The Common Sense Guide to Purchasing a Home in Good Times and Bad"

Biography

Dan Craddock has lived and worked in many parts of the world including communist and Muslim controlled countries giving him an unfettered view of life and society under various forms of government. He and his wife also spent 5 years traveling around the U.S. in their motorhome and visiting with everyday people from all walks of life. His background as an IT Project Manager, a licensed Realtor and author of the book *The Common Sense Guide to Purchasing a Home in Good Times and Bad* affords him a compelling, introspective view of the world.

NOTES

[1] Brainyquote.com,
http://www.brainyquote.com/quotes/quotes/t/thomaspain100996.html

[2] Merriam-webster.com, http://www.merriam-webster.com/dictionary/common%20sense

[3] US Department of Labor, Bureau of Labor Statistics, *Employment Situation Summary*,
http://www.bls.gov/news.release/empsit.nr0.htm

[4] Ibid

[5] U.S. Department of Labor, Bureau of Labor Statistics, *Economic News Release, Table A-15. Alternative measures of labor underutilization*,
http://www.bls.gov/news.release/empsit.t15.htm

[6] Ibid

[7] Ibid

[8]Forbes, *Home Prices Are Stabilizing, Signifying a Housing Market Bottom*, Morgan Brennan, 5/9/2012,
http://www.forbes.com/sites/morganbrennan/2012/05/09/home-prices-stabilizing-signifying-a-housing-market-bottom/

[9] Politico, *EPA's greenhouse gas power grab will damage economy*, George Allen, 5/28/13,
http://www.politico.com/story/2013/05/epa-greenhouse-gas-environmental-protection-agency-91951.html

[10] USA TODAY, *4 in 5 in USA face near-poverty, no work*, Hope Yen, 7/26/2013,
http://www.usatoday.com/story/money/business/2013/07/28/americans-poverty-no-work/2594203/

[11] CMS.gov, *Ensuring the Affordable Care Act Serves the American People,*
http://www.cms.gov/cciio/index.html
[12] TrueCapitalism, *What are Schools Teaching Our Kids?*, Kelly Henry, 1,27,2012,
http://truecapitalism.org/what-are-schools-teaching-our-kids-2/
Huffington Post, *Roosevelt High School Under Fire for Communism v. Capitalism Worksheet*, 8,20,2013
http://www.huffingtonpost.com/2012/02/05/roosevelt-high-school-und_n_1255842.html

[13] Yahoo! Finance, *The World Has More Millionaires*, Brandon Ballenger, 5/31/2013,
http://finance.yahoo.com/news/world-more-millionaires-234922509.html
[14] Fidelity.com, *Fidelity Survey Finds 86 Percent of Millionaires are Self-Made*, 7/19/2012,
http://www.fidelity.com/inside-fidelity/individual-investing/fidelity-2012-millionaire-outlook
[15] Goodreads.com, *Thomas Paine>Quotes> Quotable Quote*, http://www.goodreads.com/quotes/153804-i-have-always-strenuously-supported-the-right-of-every-man
[16] Goodreads.com, *Plato>Quotes>Quotable Quote*,
https://www.goodreads.com/quotes/569670-the-price-of-apathy-towards-public-affairs-is-to-be
[17] Brainyquote.com,
http://www.brainyquote.com/quotes/quotes/h/henryford136294.html
[18] Federal Reserve.gov, Board of Governors of the Federal Reserve System, *Currency and Coin Services*,
http://www.federalreserve.gov/paymentsystems/coin_about.htm

[19] USNEWS.com, *The Right Man at the Right Time*, Victor Li, 8/19/2013,
http://www.usnews.com/opinion/articles/2013/08/19/federal-reserve-chairman-ben-bernankes-legacy-right-man-right-time

[20] Wikipedia.org, Ben Bernanke,
http://en.wikipedia.org/wiki/Ben_Bernanke

[21] Greatwatersfinancial.com, *When the Fed Speaks, Markets Listen. Should You?*, 2013,
http://www.greatwatersfinancial.com/HOT-TOPIC-When-the-Fed-Speaks,-Markets-Listen--Should-You.c4883.htm
Investopedia.com, *The Federal Reserve: Too Powerful?*, Douglas Rice, 11/25/2009,
http://www.investopedia.com/financial-edge/1109/the-federal-reserve-too-powerful.aspx

[22] Business Insider.com, *Has The Fed Abused Its Power?*, Mike Whitney, 4/29/2011,
http://www.businessinsider.com/grand-theft-benny-2011-4

[23] Federal Reserve.gov, Board of Governors of the Federal Reserve System, *Board Members*,
http://www.federalreserve.gov/aboutthefed/bios/board/bernanke.htm

[24] CNN Money, *Senate confirms Yellen as Fed Chair*, Annalyn Kurtz, 1/7/2014,
http://money.cnn.com/2014/01/06/news/economy/janet-yellen-federal-reserve/

[25] Forbes.com, The Fed After Ben: Janel Yellen, *The Challenge of Tapering And A Bloated $3.6B Balance Sheet*, Agustino Fontevecchia, 12/2/2013,
http://www.forbes.com/sites/afontevecchia/2013/12/02/the-fed-in-2014-janet-yellen-and-the-challenge-of-tapering-and-a-3-6b-balance-sheet/

[26] Federal Reserve.gov, Board of Governors of the Federal Reserve System, *Who owns the Federal Reserve?*,
http://www.federalreserve.gov/faqs/about_14986.htm
[27] Ritholtz.com, *A Look Back at the History of the Federal Reserve*, Jeffrey M. Lacker, President Federal Reserve Bank of Richmond, 8/29/2013,
http://www.ritholtz.com/blog/2013/09/a-look-back-at-the-history-of-the-federal-reserve/
[28] Ibid
[29] Ibid
[30] Minneapolisfed.org, The Federal Reserve Bank of Minneapolis, *A History of Central Banking in the United States*,
http://www.minneapolisfed.org/community_education/student/centralbankhistory/bank.cfm
[31] Federal Reserve Education.org, *The Structure of the Federal Reserve System*,
http://www.federalreserveeducation.org/about-the-fed/structure-and-functions/
[32] The New York Times.com, *Glass-Steagall Act (1933)*, 12/4/2013,
http://topics.nytimes.com/top/reference/timestopics/subjects/g/glass_steagall_act_1933/
[33] Federal Reserve education.org, *History of the Federal Reserve*,
http://www.federalreserveeducation.org/about-the-fed/history/
[34] Ibid
[35] New York University Leonard School of Business, *Dodd-Frank and the Fed*, Paul Wachtel, 7/18/2010,
http://w4.stern.nyu.edu/blogs/regulatingwallstreet/2010/07/doddfrank-and-the-fed-kermit-s.html

[36] Time Magazine, *25 People to Blame for the Financial Crisis*, http://content.time.com/time/specials/packages/article/0,28804,1877351_1877350_1877339,00.html
The American Spectator, *The True Story of the Financial Crisis*, Peter J. Wallison, 5/2011, http://spectator.org/articles/37680/true-story-financial-crisis
[37] Federal Reserve education.org, *History of the Federal Reserve*, http://www.federalreserveeducation.org/about-the-fed/history/
[38] Richmondfed.org, Federal Reserve Bank of Richmond, *A Look Back at the History of the Federal Reserve*, Jeffrey M. Lacker, 8/29/2013, http://www.richmondfed.org/press_room/speeches/president_jeff_lacker/2013/lacker_speech_20130829.cfm
[39] Ibid
[40] Mercatus Center, George Mason University, *The Federal Reserve's Expanding Regulatory Umbrella*, Hester Peirce, Robert Greene, 4/3/2013, http://mercatus.org/publication/federal-reserves-expanding-regulatory-umbrella
[41] Ibid
[42] Federal Reserve.gov, *Federal Open Market Committee*, http://www.federalreserve.gov/monetarypolicy/fomc.htm
[43] Federal Reserve.gov, *Reserve Requirements*, http://www.federalreserve.gov/monetarypolicy/reservereq.htm
[44] Federal Reserve.gov, *The Discount Rate*, http://www.federalreserve.gov/monetarypolicy/discountrate.htm

45 Ibid

46 Federal Reserve.gov, *Federal Open Market Committee*,
http://www.federalreserve.gov/monetarypolicy/fomc.htm

47 Federal Reserve.gov, *How is the Federal Reserve System structured?*,
http://www.federalreserve.gov/faqs/about_12593.htm

48 Businessinsider.com, *What Is Quantitative Easing?*, 8/9/2010,
http://www.businessinsider.com/what-is-quantitative-easing-2010-8

49 Ibid

50 Federal Reserve.gov, Board of Governors of the Federal Reserve System, *What are the Federal Reserve's large-scale asset purchases?*,
http://www.federalreserve.gov/faqs/what-are-the-federal-reserves-large-scale-asset-purchases.htm

51 Forbes.com, *Rethinking Quantitative Easing*, Bob McTeer, 11/13/2013,
http://www.forbes.com/sites/bobmcteer/2013/11/13/rethinking-quantitative-easing/

52 CNN Money, *This could be the largest Fed stimulus yet*, Annalyn Kurtz, 10/28/2013,
http://money.cnn.com/2013/10/28/news/economy/federal-reserve-qe-stimulus/

53 Bea.gov, Bureau of Economic Analysis, *Gross Domestic Product, 3rd quarter 2013 (second estimate)*,
http://www.bea.gov/newsreleases/national/gdp/gdpnewsrelease.htm

54 The Wall Street Journal.com, *America Faces the Shock of the Old, Future Economic Growth May Depend on Innovation*, Justin Lahart, 9/8/2013,

http://online.wsj.com/news/articles/SB10001424127
88732389300457905929205462o798
55 Bls.gov, *Bureau of Labor Statistics, Current
Employment Statistics – CES (National)*,
http://www.bls.gov/ces/
56 Bureau of Labor Statistics, Databases, *Labor Force
Statistics from the Current Population Survey*,
12/13/2013,
http://data.bls.gov/pdq/SurveyOutputServlet
57 Wikipedia.org, *Employment-to-population ratio*,
http://en.wikipedia.org/wiki/Labor_participation_ra
te
58 Heritage Foundation.org, *Not Looking for Work:
Why Labor Force Participation Has Fallen During
the Recession*, James Sherk, 9/5/2013,
http://www.heritage.org/research/reports/2013/09/
not-looking-for-work-why-labor-force-participation-
has-fallen-during-the-recession
59 CNN Money, *Dow hits new all-time high. Again.*,
Maureen Farrell, 3/13/2013,
http://money.cnn.com/2013/03/13/investing/stocks-
markets/
60 Economicshelp.org, *The effects of ending
quantitative easing*, Tejvan Pettinger, 6/27/2013,
http://www.economicshelp.org/blog/7645/economic
s/the-effects-of-ending-quantitative-easing/
61 Ibid
62 NPR, *Fed Says It Will Begin Tapering Off Its
Stimulus in January*, Scott Neuman, 12/18/2013,
http://www.npr.org/blogs/thetwo-
way/2013/12/18/255253296/fed-says-it-will-begin-
tapering-off-its-stimulus-in-january
63 Foxbusiness.com, *Fed's Fisher: Stock Selloff Won't
Change Tapering Plans*, Dunstan Prial, 2/3/2014,
http://www.foxbusiness.com/economy-

policy/2014/02/03/fed-fisher-stock-selloff-wont-change-tapering-plans/

64 Federal Reserve Bank of San Francisco, *Why did the Federal Reserve start paying interest on reserve balances held on deposit at the Fed? Does the Fed pay interest on required reserves, excess reserves, or both? What interest rate does the Fed pay?*, 3/2013, http://www.frbsf.org/education/publications/doctor-econ/2013/march/federal-reserve-interest-balances-reserves

65 CNN Money, *The Fed's other trillion dollar problem*, Stephen Gandel, 6/12/2013, http://finance.fortune.cnn.com/2013/06/12/federal-reserve-bank-deposits/

66 Ibid

67 Ibid

68 Ibid

69 Federal Reserve.gov, *Does the Federal Reserve ever get audited?*, http://www.federalreserve.gov/faqs/about_12784.htm

70 Goodreads.com, http://www.goodreads.com/quotes/16243-education-is-the-most-powerful-weapon-which-you-can-use

71 Department of Education, whitehouse.gov

72 Ibid

73 The Washington Times, *A public education system that cheats our children*, Armstrong Williams, 8/4/2013, http://www.washingtontimes.com/news/2013/aug/4/williams-a-public-education-system-that-cheats-our/?page=all

The Daily Beast, *Why the World is Smarter Than Us*, Dana Goldstein, 8/9/2013,

http://www.thedailybeast.com/articles/2013/08/09/why-the-world-is-smarter-than-us.html
The Heritage Foundation, *Does Spending More on Education Improve Academic Achievement?*, Dan Lips, Shanea Watkins, Ph.D and John Feming, 9/8/2008,
http://www.heritage.org/research/reports/2008/09/does-spending-more-on-education-improve-academic-achievement
Hot Air, *Test scores for NYC students drop dramatically*, Ed Morrissey, 8/8/2013,
http://hotair.com/archives/2013/08/08/test-scores-for-nyc-students-drop-dramatically/
74 Huffington Post Politics, *Bobby Jindal Blasts Department of Justice For Lawsuit Over Louisiana School Vouchers*, Rebecca Klein, 8/26/2013,
http://www.huffingtonpost.com/2013/08/26/louisiana-vouchers-lawsuit_n_3818648.html
75 Louisiana.gov, Office of the Governor, *Gov. Jindal: U.S. Dept. of Justice Attempting to Deny Equal Opportunity in Education & Take Away Parent Choice*, 8/24/2013,
http://gov.louisiana.gov/index.cfm?md=newsroom&tmp=detail&articleID=4208
76 Ibid
77 Stanford.edu, Center for Research o Education Outcomes (CREDO), *National Charter School Study 2013*, Edward Cremata, Devora Davis, Kathleen Dickey, Kristina Lawyer, Yohannes Negassi, Margaret E. Raymond, James L. Woodworth,
http://credo.stanford.edu/documents/NCSS%202013%20Final%20Draft.pdf
78 The Washington Times, *A public education system that cheats our children*, Armstrong Williams, 8/4/2013,

http://www.washingtontimes.com/news/2013/aug/4/williams-a-public-education-system-that-cheats-our/?page=all

The Daily Beast, *Why the World is Smarter Than Us*, Dana Goldstein, 8/9/2013, http://www.thedailybeast.com/articles/2013/08/09/why-the-world-is-smarter-than-us.html

The Heritage Foundation, *Does Spending More on Education Improve Academic Achievement?*, Dan Lips, Shanea Watkins, Ph.D and John Feming, 9/8/2008, http://www.heritage.org/research/reports/2008/09/does-spending-more-on-education-improve-academic-achievement

Hot Air, *Test scores for NYC students drop dramatically*, Ed Morrissey, 8/8/2013, http://hotair.com/archives/2013/08/08/test-scores-for-nyc-students-drop-dramatically/

[79] The American Presidency Project, *Richard Nixon, 66 – Special Message to the Congress on Education Reform*, 3/3/1970, http://www.presidency.ucsb.edu/ws/?pid=2895#axzz2hFOTfMP8

[80] www2.ed.gov, *Overview of the U.S. Department of Education*, 2010, http://www2.ed.gov/about/overview/focus/what.pdf

[81] AEI.org, *Federal compliance works against education policy goals*, Melissa Junge and Sheara Krvaric, 7/28/2011, http://www.aei.org/article/education/k-12/federal-compliance-works-against-education-policy-goals/

[82] Ed.gov, U.S. Department of Education, About ED: Overview and Mission Statement, https://www2.ed.gov/about/landing.jhtml

[83] Ibid

[84] Newsone for Black America, *72 Percent of Black Kids Raised By Single Parent, 25% Overall in U.S.*, 4/27/2011, http://newsone.com/1195075/children-single-parents-u-s-american/

[85] Ibid

[86] NGA.org, NGA *Center for Best Practices*, http://www.nga.org/cms/center

[87] American Federation for Children, *FACTS*, http://www.federationforchildren.org/facts

[88] NY Post.com, New York Post, *One year on the job, 13 years in rubber room earns perv teacher $1M*, Susan Edelman, 1/27/2013, http://nypost.com/2013/01/27/one-year-on-the-job-13-years-in-rubber-room-earns-perv-teacher-1m/

[89] Khan Academy.org, https://www.khanacademy.org/#search-khan-academy

[90] Khanacademy.com, KHANACADEMY FAQ, *How did Khan Academy get started?*, http://khanacademy.desk.com/customer/portal/articles/329316-how-did-khan-academy-get-started-

[91] Studymode, *Why kids Turn to Drugs*, March 2012, http://www.studymode.com/essays/Why-Kids-Turn-Drugs-38568.html

Juvenile Justice Bulletin, *Why Do Youth Join Gangs?*, August 1998, http://www.ojjdp.gov/jjbulletin/9808/why.html

National Crime Prevention Council, *Gangs and Your Child*, http://www.ncpc.org/topics/by-audience/parents/gangs-and-your-child

Globalpost, *Characteristics of Anti-Social Behavior in Children*, Kay Tang, Demand Media, http://everydaylife.globalpost.com/characteristics-antisocial-behavior-children-5090.html

[92] Wikipedia.org, Utopia,
http://en.wikipedia.org/wiki/Utopia
[93] Linkedin.com, *Disrupting the Diploma*, 9/16/2013,
http://www.linkedin.com/today/post/article/201309
16065028-1213-disrupting-the-diploma
[94] Goodreads.com,
http://www.goodreads.com/quotes/23892-i-am-for-doing-good-to-the-poor-but-i-think
[95] Photo of Food Coupon from Chrstphre Campbell,
http://www.flickr.com/photos/chrstphre/548971792
7/in/photostream/
[96] The Foundry, *Welfare: Tackling the Fastest-Growing Part of Government Spending*, Rachel Sheffield, 4/20/2012,
http://blog.heritage.org/2012/04/20/welfare-tackling-the-fastest-growing-part-of-government-spending/
[97] Cato Institute, *The Work Versus Welfare Trade-Off: 2013*, Michael Tanner and Charles Hughes, 8/19,2013, http://www.cato.org/publications/white-paper/work-versus-welfare-trade
[98] Ibid
[99] Ibid
[100] Center on Budget and Policy Priorities, *Policy Basics: An Introduction to TANF*, Liz Schott, 12/4/2012,
http://www.cbpp.org/cms/?fa=view&id=936
[101] The Weekly Standard, *Over 100 Million Now Receiving Federal Welfare*, Daniel Halper, 9/8/2012,
http://www.weeklystandard.com/blogs/over-100-million-now-receiving-federal-welfare_649589.html
[102] USDA, *Supplemental Nutrition Assistance Program (SNAP)*, http://www.fns.usda.gov/snap/

[103] USDA, *USDA Accomplishments 2009-2012*, http://www.usda.gov/documents/Results-Nutrition.pdf

[104] The Foundry, *President Obama admits Welfare Encourages Dependency*, Rachel Sheffield, 7/9/2011, http://blog.heritage.org/2011/07/09/president-obama-admits-welfare-encourages-dependency/

Fiscal Research Center Georgia State University, *The Incentives Created by the Tax-Benefit System Facing Low-Income Families in Georgia*, Chelsea Coleman, Kendon Darlington, Mark Rider, Morgan Sinclair, February 2013, http://aysps.gsu.edu/sites/default/files/documents/Rpt%20258FIN.pdf

CNN, *Why the U.S. has a culture of dependency*, Matthew Spalding, 9/21/2012, http://www.cnn.com/2012/09/21/opinion/spalding-welfare-state-dependency

Reason.com, *How Government Handouts Foster Dependency*, John Stossel, 1/9/2013, http://reason.com/archives/2013/01/09/how-government-handouts-foster-dependenc

[105] Dwss.nv.gov, *SNAP / TANF – Electronic Benefits Transfer (EBT)*, https://dwss.nv.gov/EBT.html

[106] WWSB My Suncoast, *103 arrest warrants issued after undercover operation for EBT card fraud*, 8/21/2013, http://www.mysuncoast.com/news/manatee_newsroom/arrest-warrants-issued-after-undercover-operation-for-ebt-card-fraud/article_afeb2c08-b28a-11e2-9d41-001a4bcf6878.html

Bankers Online.com, *Food Stamp Fraud Using Electronic Benefit Transfer Cards*, http://www.bankersonline.com/security/sar/foodstampfraud.html

Boston's NPR news station 90.9 Wbur, *Mass. Audit: Welfare Benefits Paid To 1,164 Dead People*, Bob Salsberg, 5/28/2013,
http://www.wbur.org/2013/05/28/massachusetts-welfare-audit

[107] The Daily Beast.com, *JP Morgan's Food Stamp Empire*, Peter Schweizer, 10/1/12,
http://www.thedailybeast.com/articles/2012/10/01/jp-morgan-s-food-stamp-empire.html

[108] WWSB My Suncoast, *103 arrest warrants issued after undercover operation for EBT card fraud*, 8/21/2013,
http://www.mysuncoast.com/news/manatee_newsroom/arrest-warrants-issued-after-undercover-operation-for-ebt-card-fraud/article_afeb2c08-b28a-11e2-9d41-001a4bcf6878.html

Bankers Online.com, *Food Stamp Fraud Using Electronic Benefit Transfer Cards*,
http://www.bankersonline.com/security/sar/foodstampfraud.html

Boston's NPR news station 90.9 Wbur, *Mass. Audit: Welfare Benefits Paid To 1,164 Dead People*, Bob Salsberg, 5/28/2013,
http://www.wbur.org/2013/05/28/massachusetts-welfare-audit

[109] Watchdog.org, *EBT fraud and abuse: Looking past your state*, Todd Shepherd, 7/24/2012,
http://watchdog.org/43198/ebt-fraud-and-abuse-looking-past-your-state/

[110] USDA, *The Extent of Trafficking in the Supplemental Nutrition Assistance Program: 2009-2011(Summary)*, 8/2013,
http://www.fns.usda.gov/ORA/menu/Published/SNAP/FILES/ProgramIntegrity/Trafficking2009_Summary.pdf

[111] Ibid

[112] Ibid

[113] AZCentral.com, *Over $600,000 seized in Phoenix food-stamp fraud probe*, Sydney Schuman, 8/29/2013, http://www.azcentral.com/community/phoenix/articles/20130829men-arrested-phoenix-food-stamps-fraud-abrk.html

[114] Payne, Ruby K. (2005) *A Framework for Understanding Poverty 4th Edition*, Highlands, TX, aha! Process, Inc.

[115] U.S. Government Accountability Office, *2012 Annual Report Opportunities to Reduce Duplication, Overlap and Fragmentation*, Achieve Savings, and Enhance Revenue, 2/28/2012, http://www.gao.gov/products/GAO-12-342SP
The Washington Post, *Government Overlap costs taxpayers billions, GAO reports*, Ed O'Keefe, 3/1/2011, http://voices.washingtonpost.com/federal-eye/2011/03/government_overlap_costs_taxpa.html
GAO, 2013 Annual Duplication Report GAO-13-279SP, *Actions Needed to Reduce Fragmentation, Overlap, and Duplication, and Achieve Financial Benefits*, 7/15/2003, http://www.agacgfm.org/AGA/PDC2013/presentations/M101---Davis.pdf

[116] Training Magazine, *Training magazine Ranks 2012 Top 125 Organizations*, 2/14/2012, http://www.trainingmag.com/article/training-magazine-ranks-2012-top-125-organizations
AOL Jobs, *On-The-Job Training: Jobs That Require No College Degree*, David Schepp, 2/13/2012, http://jobs.aol.com/articles/2012/02/13/on-the-job-training-jobs-that-require-no-college-degree-infogr/
Seedco, http://www.seedco.org/

[117] Brainyquote.com,
http://www.brainyquote.com/quotes/quotes/m/mittr omney415551.html
[118] Treasury Direct, *Interest Expense on the Debt Outstanding*,
http://www.treasurydirect.gov/govt/reports/ir/ir_ex pense.htm
[119] Ibid
[120] Center on Budget and Policy Priorities, *Sequestration by the Numbers*, Richard Kogan, 3/22/2013,
http://www.cbpp.org/cms/?fa=view&id=3937
[121] Treasury Direct, *Interest Expense on the Debt Outstanding*,
http://www.treasurydirect.gov/govt/reports/ir/ir_ex pense.htm
[122] Huffingtonpost.com, *Sequestration Victims Happy With A Budget Deal That Relieves A Third Of The Cuts*, Sam Stein, 12/11/2013,
http://www.huffingtonpost.com/2013/12/11/sequeste r-victims-_n_4425673.html
[123] Whitehouse.gov, *TooManyWebsites.gov*, Macon Phillips, 6/13/2011,
http://www.whitehouse.gov/blog/2011/06/13/tooma nywebsitesgov
[124] FedSpending.org, *New Data Released on FedSpending.org*, http://www.fedspending.org/
[125] UShistory.org, American Government, *8d. Reforming the Bureaucracy*,
http://www.ushistory.org/gov/8d.asp
[126] Globe-Net, *To Compete Successfully, Companies Must Change*, 2/9/2012, http://www.globe-net.com/articles/2012/february/11/to-compete-successfully,-companies-must-change/

[127] Brainyquote.com,
http://www.brainyquote.com/quotes/quotes/a/abrah
amlin143183.html
[128] National Debt Clock,
http://www.usdebtclock.org/#
[129] Ibid
[130] The New York Times, *Lingering Confusion in Debt Ceiling Deal's Temporary Fix*, Anne Lowrey, 10/17/2013,
http://www.nytimes.com/2013/10/18/business/econ
omy/lingering-confusion-in-debt-ceiling-deals-
temporary-
fix.html?adxnnl=1&ref=nationaldebtus&adxnnlx=138
2118896-DQcZSXmkgIVPlzHFOmNmvQ
[131] ABCNews.com, *Obama Signs Debt Ceiling Measure Into Law*, Darlene Superville, 2/16/2014,
http://abcnews.go.com/Politics/wireStory/obama-
signs-debt-ceiling-measure-law-22535852
[132] US Debt Clock, http://www.usdebtclock.org/
[133] Factcheck.org, *Spinning Obama's Budget*, 4/2013,
http://www.factcheck.org/2013/04/spinning-
obamas-budget/
[134] Ibid
[135] The Washington Times, *Obama's national debt rate on track to double*, Dave Boyer, 10/9/2013,
http://www.washingtontimes.com/news/2013/oct/9/
obamas-national-debt-rate-on-track-to-double/
[136] CBS News, *National Debt has increased more under Obama than under Bush*, Mark Knoller, 3/19/2012, http://www.cbsnews.com/8301-
503544_162-57400369-503544/national-debt-has-
increased-more-under-obama-than-under-bush/
[137] Ibid
[138] Townhall.com, *Who Really Owns the U.S. National Debt?*, 1/21/2013,

http://finance.townhall.com/columnists/politicalcalculations/2013/01/21/who-really-owns-the-us-national-debt-n1493555/page/full

[139] CHINADAILY USA, *Replace dollar with supper currency: economist*, Michael Barris and Eu Jing and Chen Jia, 1/29/2014, http://usa.chinadaily.com.cn/world/2014-01/29/content_17264069.htm

[140] Treasury Direct, *Interest Expense on the Debt Outstanding*, http://www.treasurydirect.gov/govt/reports/ir/ir_expense.htm

[141] Board of Governors of the Federal Reserve System, *Why are interest rates being kept at a low level?*, http://www.federalreserve.gov/faqs/money_12849.htm

[142] CNSNews.com, *CBO: Federal Revenue to Set Record in 2013*, Matt Cover, 2/7/2013, http://cnsnews.com/news/article/cbo-federal-revenue-set-record-2013

[143] CNN Money, *How Obama's tax hikes would hit the rich and middle class*, Jeanne Sahadi, 4/23/2013, http://money.cnn.com/2013/04/23/pf/taxes/obama-taxes/

[144] Heritage Organization, Federal Budget in Pictures, *Top 10 Percent of Earners Paid Majority of US Tax Percentage*, http://www.heritage.org/federalbudget/top10-percent-income-earners

[145] Treasury Direct, *Gift Contributions to Reduce Debt Held by the Public*, http://www.treasurydirect.gov/govt/reports/pd/gift/gift.htm

[146] Ibid

[147] USAtoday.com, *Should GM repay $10B rescue cost? CEO says no*, Todd Spangler, 12/17/2013, http://www.usatoday.com/story/money/cars/2013/12/16/general-motors-gm-bailout-repayment/4043607/

[148] CBS News, *Somebody Stop The "Bailout Party"*, Declan McCullagh, 9/10/2009, http://www.cbsnews.com/2100-503363_162-4891193.html

[149] FTC, *FTC Fact Sheet: Antitrust Laws: A Brief History*, http://www.ftc.gov/bcp/edu/microsites/youarehere/pages/pdf/FTC-Competition_Antitrust-Laws.pdf

[150] The Washington Post, *Before Solyndra, a long history of failed government energy projects*, Steven Mufson, 11/11/2011, http://articles.washingtonpost.com/2011-11-11/news/35282864_1_new-energy-technology-energy-industry-river-reactor

[151] The Wall Street Journal, *The Venture Capital Secret: 3 Out of 4 Start-Ups Fail*, Deborah Gage, 9/20/2012, http://online.wsj.com/news/articles/SB10000872396390443720204578004980476429190

[152] Quotationspage.com, http://www.quotationspage.com/quote/28911.html

[153] Family Guardian, *Do Gun Laws Reduce Crime?*, http://famguardian.org/Subjects/GunControl/Articles/GUNLAWS.TXT

[154] Guns Save Lives, *GOA's Fact Sheet: Guns Save Lives*, 9/17/2009, http://guns-save-lives.com/?s=fact+sheet&x=16&y=10

[155] Washington Post, *Killings in line of duty haunt police officers*, 2/9/2012, http://articles.washingtonpost.com/2012-02-

09/local/35443106_1_fatal-police-shootings-police-officers-bank-robber

[156] [156] Guns Save Lives, *GOA's Fact Sheet: Guns Save Lives,* 9/17/2009, http://guns-save-lives.com/?s=fact+sheet&x=16&y=10

[157] Archives.gov, *Bill of Rights,* http://www.archives.gov/exhibits/charters/bill_of_rights_transcript.html

[158] U.S. Department of Health & Human Services, ASPE Fact Sheet, *Youth from Low-Income Families,* 7/2009, http://aspe.hhs.gov/hsp/09/vulnerableyouth/3/index.shtml

The University of Oklahoma, *Does income inequality lead to more crime? A comparison of cross-sectional and time-series analyses of United States counties,* Jesse Brush, 7/11/2006, http://www.ou.edu/cls/online/lstd2333/pdfs/unit4_income_inequality.pdf

[159] The White House, *Real #DrugPolicyReform: DOJ's Change in Mandatory Minimum Policies,* Rafael Lemaitre, 8/12/2013, http://www.whitehouse.gov/blog/2013/08/12/real-drugpolicyreform-doj-s-change-mandatory-minimum-policies

[160] Policymic, *Marijuana Legalization: Colorado and Washington State Grapple With Implementing New Laws,* Ella Peterson, http://www.policymic.com/articles/22459/marijuana-legalization-colorado-and-washington-state-grapple-with-implementing-new-laws

[161] Brainyquote.com, http://www.brainyquote.com/quotes/quotes/e/edmundburk379415.html

[162] The Hill, *Poll: 72 Percent of small businesses say regulations are hurting them*, Ben Goad, 1/25/2013, http://thehill.com/blogs/regwatch/business/279443-poll-72-percent-of-small-businesses-say-regulations-are-hurting-

[163] CBS News, *U.S. Workers World's Most Productive*, 2/11/2009, http://www.cbsnews.com/2100-500395_162-3228735.html

[164] U.S. Bureau of Labor Statistics, *International Labor Comparisons*, 5/2013, http://www.bls.gov/spotlight/2013/ilc/pdf/international-labor-comparisons.pdf

[165] CNN Money, *CEO pay is 380 times average worker's – AFL-CIO*, 4/19/2012, http://money.cnn.com/2012/04/19/news/economy/ceo-pay/index.htm

[166] Ibid

[167] Research Triangle Business Advisors, Bob De Contreras, *What Does a CEO DO?*, http://www.rt-ba.com/research-articles-leadership-ceodo.html

[168] TheUSAonline.com, *Economy, Impact of the World Economy*, http://www.theusaonline.com/economy/world-economy.htm

[169] Roanoketrade.com, *Outsourcing Overseas and its Effect on the US Economy*, Madison Correnti, http://www.roanoketrade.com/post/Correnti_essay.pdf

[170] Huffington Post, *11 American Companies That Brought Jobs Back Home*, Harry Bradford, 5/31/2013, http://www.huffingtonpost.com/2013/05/31/companies-us-jobs-reshoring_n_3340278.html

[171] The Independent Institute, *Sweatshops and Third World Living Standards: Are the Jobs Worth the*

Sweat?, 9/27/2004,
http://www.independent.org/publications/working_papers/article.asp?id=1369

[172] [172] Huffington Post, *11 American Companies That Brought Jobs Back Home*, Harry Bradford, 5/31/2013,
http://www.huffingtonpost.com/2013/05/31/companies-us-jobs-reshoring_n_3340278.html

[173] Wikipedia, *Financial crisis of 2007-08*,
http://en.wikipedia.org/wiki/Financial_crisis_of_2007%E2%80%9308

[174] Reuters, *The Great Debate, Fixing 'too-big-to-fail'*, Richard Stallman, 2/4/2013,
http://blogs.reuters.com/great-debate/tag/anti-trust-law/

[175] Banking.senate.gov, *BRIEF SUMMARY OF THE DODD-FRANK WALL STREET REFORM AND CONSUMER PROTECTION ACT*,
http://www.banking.senate.gov/public/_files/070110_Dodd_Frank_Wall_Street_Reform_comprehensive_summary_Final.pdf

[176] CBSNews.com, *Mass Layoffs Plump CEO Pockets*, Ann Binlot, 9/1/2013,
http://www.cbsnews.com/8300-503983_162-503983.html?keyword=CEO+Salary

[177] iClarified, *Apple Changes Tim Cook's Compensation, Makes it Performance Based*, 6/22/2013, http://www.iclarified.com/31346/apple-changes-tim-cooks-compensation-makes-it-performance-based

[178] Dealbook.NYTimes.com, *Hedge Fund Titans' Pay Stretching to 10 Figures*, Julie Creswell, 4/15/2013, http://dealbook.nytimes.com/2013/04/15/pay-stretching-to-10-figures/?_r=0

[179] The Washington Post, *Do private-sector unions still have a future in the U.S.?*, Brad Plumer, 6/13/2013, http://www.washingtonpost.com/blogs/wonkblog/wp/2013/06/13/do-private-sector-unions-still-have-a-future-in-the-u-s/

[180] University of California Santa Cruz, G. William Domhoff, *The Rise and Fall of Labor Unions in The U.S.*, http://www2.ucsc.edu/whorulesamerica/power/history_of_labor_unions.html

[181] The New York Times, *Strained States Turning to Laws to Curb Labor Unions*, Steven Greenhouse, 1/3/2011, http://www.nytimes.com/2011/01/04/business/04labor.html?pagewanted=all

[182] Ibid

[183] UNIONFACTS.COM, *Examples of Union Threats, Violence, and Intimidation*, 3/10/2011, http://www.unionfacts.com/article/crime-and-corruption/examples-of-union-threats-violence-and-intimidation/

Frontpagemag.com, *Union Violence and Mob Mayhem in Michigan*, Arnold Ahlert, 12/12/2012, http://frontpagemag.com/2012/arnold-ahlert/union-violence-and-mob-mayhem-in-michigan/

National Institute For Labor Relations Research, http://nilrr.org/resources/violence-event-data-file/

[184] SEIU.org, *Political Director for SEIU 1199 NW / Renton WA*, https://careers-seiu.icims.com/jobs/1648/political-director-for-seiu-1199-nw---renton-wa/job

The Wall Street Journal Online, *Political Spending by Unions Far Exceeds Direct Donations*, 7/10/2012,

http://online.wsj.com/article/SB1000142405270230
4782404577488584031850026.html

[185] Anchorage Daily News, *Compass: Unions still needed, but old thinking won't save them*, Gregory Fisher, 9/31/2013,
http://www.adn.com/2013/08/31/3051921/compass-unions-still-needed-but.html

[186] ABC News, *Where Do Unions Stand on Immigration Reform?*, Ted Hesson, 1/23/2013,
http://abcnews.go.com/ABC_Univision/Politics/unions-stand-immigration-reform/story?id=18288148

[187] Policymic, *Hostess Bankruptcy: One Big Win for Labor Unions, One Big Loss for Laborers*, James Street,
http://www.policymic.com/articles/19155/hostess-bankruptcy-one-big-win-for-labor-unions-one-big-loss-for-laborers
ABC News, *Hostess Reopening Plants, Without Union Workers*, 4/26/2013,
http://abcnews.go.com/Business/twinkies-return-hostess-unions/story?id=19043854

[188] Ibid

[189] Globalpost.com, *Workers and management cause demise of Hostess*, Michael Kelly, 11/16/2012,
http://www.globalpost.com/dispatch/news/business/companies/121116/hostess-bankruptcy-twinkies#1

[190] Reuters.com, *Loss at Volkswagen plant upends union's plan for U.S. South*, Bernie Woodall, 2/15/2014,
http://www.reuters.com/article/2014/02/15/us-autos-vw-election-idUSBREA1D1DP20140215

[191] Goodquotes.com,
http://www.goodquotes.com/quote/marty-meehan/real-lobbying-reform-must-end-the-prac

[192] Business Pundit, *10 of the Biggest Lobbies in Washington*, Gerri, 4/26/2011, http://www.businesspundit.com/10-of-the-biggest-lobbies-in-washington/

[193] Brainyquote.com, http://www.brainyquote.com/quotes/quotes/f/franklind403816.html

[194] Center for American Progress, *Voter Suppression 101, How Conservatives Are Conspiring to Disenfranchise Millions of Americans*, Scott Keyes, Ian Millhiser, Tobin Van Ostern, and Abraham White, 4/4/2012, http://www.americanprogress.org/issues/progressive-movement/report/2012/04/04/11380/voter-suppression-101/

[195] Huffington Post Politics, *Black Voter Turnout Rate Passes Whites in 2012 Election*, Hope Yen, 4/28/2013, http://www.huffingtonpost.com/2013/04/28/black-voter-turnout-2012-election_n_3173673.html

[196] International Business Times, *Why is There so Much Voter Apathy in U.S. Elections?*, 9/19/2011, http://www.ibtimes.com/why-there-so-much-voter-apathy-us-elections-315494

[197] Wikipedia, *Voting rights in the United States*, http://en.wikipedia.org/wiki/Voting_rights_in_the_United_States

[198] National Policy Analysis, Horace Cooper, *Voter Fraud is Real: Why the Voting Rights Act Should Be Used to Fight Election Fraud*, 8/2012, http://www.nationalcenter.org/NPA636.html

[199] Brennan Center for Justice at the New York University School of Law, *MYTH OF VOTER FRAUD*, http://www.brennancenter.org/issues/voter-fraud

[200] Ourgeneration.org,
http://ourgeneration.org/term-limits/
[201] Wikipedia, *Twenty-second Amendment to the United States Constitution*,
http://en.wikipedia.org/wiki/Twenty-second_Amendment_to_the_United_States_Constitution
[202] Examiner.com, *Congress: it was never meant to be a career*, 1/12/2012,
http://www.examiner.com/article/congress-it-was-never-meant-to-be-a-career
[203] Brainyquote.com,
http://www.brainyquote.com/quotes/quotes/m/marcorubio430120.html
[204] Pew Research Center, *Unauthorized Immigrants: How Pew Research Counts Them and What We Know About Them*, 4/17/2013,
http://www.pewresearch.org/2013/04/17/unauthorized-immigrants-how-pew-research-counts-them-and-what-we-know-about-them/
[205] Udall Center for studies in Public Policy, University of Arizona, Judith Gans, *Illegal Immigration to the United States Causes and Policy Solutions*,
http://udallcenter.arizona.edu/immigration/publications/fact_sheet_no_3_illegal_immigration.pdf
[206] The Washington Post, *Is our border security working? It's far from clear.*, Suzy Khimm, 1/30/2013,
http://www.washingtonpost.com/blogs/wonkblog/wp/2013/01/30/is-our-border-security-working-its-far-from-clear/
American Thinker, *Federal enforcement, not Immigration Reform, is Needed*, Michael Bargo, Jr., 5/4/2013,

http://www.americanthinker.com/2013/05/federal_e
nforcement_not_immigration_reform_is_needed.ht
ml

[207] Cornell University Law School, *U.S. Constitution 14th Amendment*,
http://www.law.cornell.edu/constitution/amendment
xiv

[208] Federalistblog.us, *Historical Analysis of the Meaning of the 14th Amendment's First Section*, P.A. Madison, 8/2/2010,
http://www.federalistblog.us/mt/articles/14th_dum
my_guide.htm

[209] Rock Center with Brian Williams, *Born in the U.S.A.: Birth tourists get instant U.S. citizenship for their newborns*, Anna Schecter, 10/28/2011,
http://rockcenter.nbcnews.com/_news/2011/10/28/
8511587-born-in-the-usa-birth-tourists-get-instant-
us-citizenship-for-their-newborns

[210] Rock Center with Brian Williams, *Born in the U.S.A.: Birth tourists get instant U.S. citizenship for their newborns*, Anna Schecter, 10/28/2011,
http://rockcenter.nbcnews.com/_news/2011/10/28/
8511587-born-in-the-usa-birth-tourists-get-instant-
us-citizenship-for-their-newborns?lite

[211] CBS News, *"Maternity Tourism": How Chinese couples buy U.S. citizenship for their babies*, John Blackstone, 1/28/2013,
http://www.cbsnews.com/8301-18563_162-
57566313/maternity-tourism-how-chinese-couples-
buy-u.s-citizenship-for-their-babies/

[212] The New York Times, *Taking More Seats on Campus, Foreigners Also Pay the Freight*, Tamar Lewin, 2/4/2012,
http://www.nytimes.com/2012/02/05/education/int

ernational-students-pay-top-dollar-at-us-colleges.html

[213] Federalistblog.us, *Historical Analysis of the Meaning of the 14th Amendment's First Section*, P.A. Madison, 8/2/2010, http://www.federalistblog.us/mt/articles/14th_dum my_guide.htm

[214] National Archives, *The Constitutional Amendment Process*, http://www.archives.gov/federal-register/constitution/

[215] Federalistblog.us, *Historical Analysis of the Meaning of the 14th Amendment's First Section*, P.A. Madison, 8/2/2010, http://www.federalistblog.us/mt/articles/14th_dum my_guide.htm

[216] The New York Times, *Number of Illegal Immigrants in the U.S. May Be on Rise Again, Estimates Say*, Julia Preston, 10/23/2013, http://www.nytimes.com/2013/09/24/us/immigrant -population-shows-signs-of-growth-estimates-show.html?_r=0

[217] Deseret News, *Rep. Eric Cantor: Why do we educate foreigners and force them to go back home?*, Rep. Eric Cantor, 11/30/2012, http://www.deseretnews.com/article/765616695/Wh y-do-we-educate-foreigners-and-force-them-to-go-back-home.html

[218] Welcome to USA.gov, *Government Benefits*, http://www.welcometousa.gov/Government_benefits /default.htm

[219] Ibid

[220] Ibid

[221] Inc.com, *Guest Speaker: The Root Causes of Immigration*, Kevin Boyle, 3/1/2007,

http://www.inc.com/magazine/20070301/column-guest.html

[222] US Immigration.com, *Illegal Immigrants Coming In Through Canada,* http://www.usimmigration.com/illegal-immigrants-through-canada.html

[223] The Boston Globe, *America's borders, porous from the start,* Peter Andreas, 3/3/2013, http://www.bostonglobe.com/ideas/2013/03/03/america-borders-porous-from-start/OUF92CcYcpCFbAeruuKwKO/story.html

[224] The Huffington Post, *Passing Immigration Reform is Now a Humanitarian Necessity,* Marisa Trevino, 9/25/2010, http://www.huffingtonpost.com/marisa-trevi/passing-immigration-refor_b_694900.html

[225] Federalistblog.us, *Historical Analysis of the Meaning of the 14th Amendment's First Section,* P.A. Madison, 8/2/2010, http://www.federalistblog.us/mt/articles/14th_dummy_guide.htm

[226] Brainyquote.com, http://www.brainyquote.com/quotes/quotes/c/carlyfiori455304.html

[227] National Geographic.com, *Border Wars,* http://channel.nationalgeographic.com/channel/border-wars/

[228] American Thinker.com, *The Drug Cartels Keep Arizona's Border Wide Open,* Leo W. Banks, 5/7/2012, http://www.americanthinker.com/2012/05/the_drug_cartels_keep_arizonas_border_wide_open.html

[229] CNS News.com, *Napolitano: Terrorists Enter U.S. from Mexico 'From Time to Time',* Edwin Mora, 7/30/2012,

http://cnsnews.com/news/article/napolitano-terrorists-enter-us-mexico-time-time

[230] CNN.com, *Report: U.S.-Canada border security lacking*, 2/1/2011, http://www.cnn.com/2011/POLITICS/02/01/u.s..canadian.border/

[231] Federation for American Immigration Reform, *Visa Overstayers (2013)*, http://www.fairus.org/issue/visa-overstayers

[232] Homeland Security, *"Visa Security and Overstays: How Secure is America?"*, 5/21/2013, http://www.dhs.gov/news/2013/05/21/written-testimony-ice-cbp-and-nppd-house-homeland-security-subcommittee-border-and

[233] Fox News, *Boston probe sheds light on 'astonishing' problems in student visa system*, Barnini Chakraborty, 5/7/2013, http://www.foxnews.com/politics/2013/05/07/boston-probe-problems-student-visa-overstays/

[234] Federation for American Immigration Reform, *Visa Overstayers (2013)*, http://www.fairus.org/issue/visa-overstayers

[235] Federation for American Immigration Reform, *Illegal Immigration is a Crime (2013)*, http://www.fairus.org/issue/illegal-immigration-is-a-crime

[236] Ibid

[237] American Patrol.com, *Illegal Immigration is a Crime*, http://www.americanpatrol.com/REFERENCE/isacrime.html

[238] The Washington Times, *Mexico's illegals laws tougher than Arizona's*, Jerry Seper, 5/3/2010, http://www.washingtontimes.com/news/2010/may/

03/mexicos-illegals-laws-tougher-than-arizonas/?page=all

Foreign Policy.com, *The World's Worst Immigration Laws*, Peter Williams, 4/29/2010, http://www.foreignpolicy.com/articles/2010/04/29/the_world_s_worst_immigration_laws

239 Constitutionus.com, *The United States Constitution*, http://constitutionus.com/

240 The Washington Times, *Mexico's illegals laws tougher than Arizona's*, Jerry Seper, 5/3/2010, http://www.washingtontimes.com/news/2010/may/03/mexicos-illegals-laws-tougher-than-arizonas/?page=all

241 The New York Times, *Arizona Sues Federal Government for Failing to Enforce Immigration*, Marc Lacey and Salvador Rodriquez, 2/10/2011, http://thecaucus.blogs.nytimes.com/2011/02/10/arizona-plans-to-sue-federal-government/?_r=0

HG.org, Legal Resources, *What is Immigration Law?*, http://www.hg.org/immigration-law.html

242 Goodreads.com, https://www.goodreads.com/quotes/92116-we-contend-that-for-a-nation-to-try-to-tax

243 TownhallFinance.com, *How Many Pages Long Is the U.S. Income Tax Code in 2013?*, 2/17/2013, http://finance.townhall.com/columnists/politicalcalculations/2013/02/17/how-many-pages-long-is-the-us-income-tax-code-in-2013-n1514277

244 Cato Institute, *10 Outrageous Facts About the Income Tax*, Chris Edwards, 4/15/2003, http://www.cato.org/publications/commentary/10-outrageous-facts-about-income-tax

245 Mercatus Center George Mason University, Antony Davies, *Corporate Taxes Trickle Down*, 4/2/2012,

http://mercatus.org/expert_commentary/corporate-taxes-trickle-down

246 Jonathan Turley, *Wealthy "Faux Farmers" Get Huge Agricultural Tax Breaks on Their Properties*, Elaine Magliaro, 4/17/2011, http://jonathanturley.org/2011/04/17/wealthy-%E2%80%9Cfaux-farmers%E2%80%9D-get-huge-agricultural-tax-breaks-on-their-properties/ Huffington Post, *Shocker: Huge Companies Cost U.S. Billions Exploiting Tax Break Designed for Farmers Swapping Horses*, Ian Reifowitz, 1/8/2013, http://www.huffingtonpost.com/ian-reifowitz/tax-loopholes_b_2425012.html

247 CNN Money, *Actavis: The latest Fortune 500 company to "leave" the U.S. for tax reasons*, Brian O'Keefe, 5/21/2013, http://features.blogs.fortune.cnn.com/2013/05/21/actavis-the-latest-fortune-500-company-to-leave-the-u-s-for-tax-reasons/

248 Ibid

249 Ibid

250 FairTax.org, *The FairTax Plan Your Money, Your Decision*, http://www.fairtax.org/site/PageServer?pagename=HowFairTaxWorks

251 Ibid

252 FairTax.org, *The FairTax prebate explained*, http://www.fairtax.org/PDF/PrebateExplained.pdf

253 Ibid

254 Investopedia, *Flat Tax*, http://www.investopedia.com/terms/f/flattax.asp

255 Forbes.com, *What is a Flat Tax? (Surprise! It is a VAT)*, Len Burman, 10/24/2011, http://www.forbes.com/sites/leonardburman/2011/10/24/what-is-a-flat-tax-surprise-it-is-a-vat/

[256] Business Insider, 17 *Great American Companies That Keep Mountains of Cash Overseas Just Like Apple Does*, Walter Hickey, 5/21/2013, http://www.businessinsider.com/apple-google-microsoft-coca-cola-taxes-cash-offshore-2013-5

[257] Forbes.com, *Apple, Google Among Top U.S. Companies Parking Cash Offshore To Reduce Taxes, Study Says*, Connie Guglielmo, 8/1/2013, http://www.forbes.com/sites/connieguglielmo/2013/08/01/apple-google-among-top-u-s-companies-parking-cash-offshore-to-reduce-taxes-study-says/

[258] BloombergBusinessweek, *To Tax, or Not to Tax, Overseas Cash Hoards*, Elizabeth Dwoskin, 10/10/2012, http://www.businessweek.com/articles/2012-10-10/to-tax-or-not-to-tax-overseas-cash-hoards

[259] Ibid

[260] Forbes.com, *Apple, Google Among Top U.S. Companies Parking Cash Offshore To Reduce Taxes, Study Says*, Connie Guglielmo, 8/1/2013, http://www.forbes.com/sites/connieguglielmo/2013/08/01/apple-google-among-top-u-s-companies-parking-cash-offshore-to-reduce-taxes-study-says/

[261] Brainyquote.com, http://www.brainyquote.com/quotes/quotes/j/jimryun355955.html

[262] Center on Budget and Policy Priorities, *Policy Basics: Where Do Our Federal Tax Dollars Go?*, 4/12/2013, http://www.cbpp.org/cms/?fa=view&id=1258

[263] The Daily Caller, *Report: Federal unfunded liabilities total $84 trillion*, Michael Bastasch, 7/16/2012, http://dailycaller.com/2012/07/16/report-federal-unfunded-liabilities-total-84-trillion/

264 Mercatus.org, Mercatus Center, George Mason University, *The US Debt in Perspective*, Veronique de Rugy, 7/16/2013, http://mercatus.org/publication/us-debt-perspective

265 Congressional Budget Office, *CBO's 2011 Long-Term Projections for Social Security: Infographic*, http://www.cbo.gov/publication/41139

266 Ibid

267 Ibid

268 Ibid

269 Ibid

270 Heritage.org, *Federal Budget in Pictures*, http://www.heritage.org/federalbudget/entitlement-spending-double

271 Congressional Budget Office, *CBO's 2011 Long-Term Projections for Social Security: Infographic*, http://www.cbo.gov/publication/41139

272 KARE 11, *Why American's say they are working longer*, 11/5/2013, http://www.kare11.com/news/money/article/1026750/329/Why-Americans-say-they-are-working-longer

273 Obamacare facts.com, *Obamacare Medicare: Obamacare and Medicare*, http://obamacarefacts.com/obamacare-medicare.php

274 GAO, *Medicare and Medicaid Fraud, Waste, and Abuse: Effective Implementation of Recent Laws and Agency Actions Could Help Reduce Improper Payments*, 5/9/2011, http://www.gao.gov/products/GAO-11-409T

275 Monticello.org, http://www.monticello.org/site/jefferson/government-big-enough-to-give-you-everything-you-wantquotation

276 Yahoo! Voices, *Amity Shlaes 'Coolidge' About the Last President to Cut the Size of Government*, Mark

Whittington, 5/8/2013,
http://voices.yahoo.com/amity-shlaes-coolidge-last-president-to-12119319.html?cat=37
[277] Forbes, *The Growth of Government: 1980 To 2012*, Mike Patton, 1/24/2013,
http://www.forbes.com/sites/mikepatton/2013/01/24/the-growth-of-the-federal-government-1980-to-2012/
[278] Whitehouse.gov, *Regulation Reform*,
http://www.whitehouse.gov/21stcenturygov/actions/21st-century-regulatory-system
[279] Ibid
[280] Cato Institute, *Regulatory Process Reform From Ford to Clinton*, Murray Weidenbaum,
http://www.cato.org/sites/cato.org/files/serials/files/regulation/1991/1/reg20n1a.html
[281] Small Businesses for Sensible Regulations,
http://www.sensibleregulations.org/resources/facts-and-figures/
[282] Zerohedge.com, *The Cost of Government Regulation: $1.75 Trillion*, Tyler Durden, 7/22/2012,
http://www.zerohedge.com/news/cost-government-regulation-175-trillion
[283] Economic Research, Federal Reserve Bank of St. Louis, *Corporate Profits After Tax (without IVA and CCAdj) (CP)*,
http://research.stlouisfed.org/fred2/series/CP/
[284] Office of the Federal Register, *A Guide to the Rulemaking Process*,
https://www.federalregister.gov/uploads/2011/01/the_rulemaking_process.pdf
[285] Ibid
[286] Washington Post, The Fact Checker, *How many pages of regulations for 'Obamacare'?*, Glenn Kessler, 5/15/2013,

http://www.washingtonpost.com/blogs/fact-checker/post/how-many-pages-of-regulations-for-obamacare/2013/05/14/61eec914-bcf9-11e2-9b09-1638acc3942e_blog.html
287 Forbes, *Delay of Obamacare's Employer Mandate Exacerbates An Already Bad Situation*, Sally Pipes, 8/5/2013, http://www.forbes.com/sites/sallypipes/2013/08/05/delay-of-obamacares-employer-mandate-exacerbates-an-already-bad-situation/
288 Harvard Business School, *Industry Self-Regulation: What's Working (and What's Not)?*, Martha Lagace, 4/9/2007, http://hbswk.hbs.edu/item/5590.html
289 The Better Business Bureau, *BBB's Industry Self-Regulation Solutions*, http://www.bbb.org/us/partnerships/self-regulation/
290 Brainyquote.com, http://www.brainyquote.com/quotes/quotes/v/virgilgood355061.html
291 Wikipedia, *United States Department of Energy*, http://en.wikipedia.org/wiki/United_States_Department_of_Energy
292 The Washington Post, *Why there's no U.S. energy policy*, 3/19/2011, http://www.washingtonpost.com/wp-dyn/content/article/2011/03/19/AR2011031904771.html
293 Energy.gov Office of Management, DOE HISTORY TIMELINE, http://energy.gov/management/office-management/operational-management/history/doe-history-timeline
294 Alliance to Save Energy, The Energy Independence and Security Act of 2007 (H.R. 6), *Summary of Key*

Provisions, http://www.ase.org/resources/energy-independence-and-security-act-2007

[295] CNN Money, *Made (again) in the USA: The return of American Manufacturing*, Nin-Hai Tseng, 6/29/2011, http://finance.fortune.cnn.com/2011/06/29/return-of-american-manufacturing/

[296] Ibid

[297] Ibid

[298] Wikipedia, *1973 oil crisis*, http://en.wikipedia.org/wiki/1973_oil_crisis
Wikipedia, *1979 energy crisis*, http://en.wikipedia.org/wiki/1979_energy_crisis

[299] The Foundry, *Matt Damon's Anti-Fracking Movie Financed by Oil-Rich Arab Nation*, Lachlan Markay, 9/28/2012, http://blog.heritage.org/2012/09/28/matt-damons-anti-fracking-movie-financed-by-oil-rich-arab-nation/

[300] PolitiFact.com, *Obama says Keystone XL would mean "maybe 2,000 jobs"*, http://www.politifact.com/truth-o-meter/statements/2013/jul/31/barack-obama/obama-says-keystone-xl-would-mean-maybe-2000-jobs/

[301] Documentcloud.org, United States Department of State Bureau of Oceans and International Environmental and Scientific Affairs, *Final Supplemental Environmental Impact Statement for the Keystone XL Project*, 1/2014, http://www.documentcloud.org/documents/1011311-keystone-report.html#document/p1

[302] AEIdeas, *US oil production grew more in 2012 than in any year in the history of the domestic oil industry back to the Civil War*, Mark J. Perry,

9/13/2013, http://www.aei-ideas.org/2013/01/us-oil-production-grew-more-in-2012-than-in-any-year-in-the-history-of-the-domestic-oil-industry-back-to-1859/

[303] Manhattan Institute for Policy Research, Energy Policy & the Environment Report, *NEW TECHNOLOGY FOR OLD FUELS: Innovation in Oil and Natural Gas Production Assures Future Supplies*, Robert Bryce, 4/12/2013, http://www.manhattan-institute.org/html/eper_12.htm#.UjNsc8aTiSp

[304] Our Finite World, *The Close Tie Between Energy Consumption, Employment, and Recession*, 9/17/2013, http://ourfiniteworld.com/2012/09/17/the-close-tie-between-energy-consumption-employment-and-recession/

[305] Pickens Plan, *Monthly Oil Imports*, http://www.pickensplan.com/oilimports/

[306] World Nuclear Association, *Nuclear Power in the USA*, 7/31/2013, http://www.world-nuclear.org/info/Country-Profiles/Countries-T-Z/USA--Nuclear-Power/#.UidouZKTiSo

[307] Ibid

[308] World Nuclear Association, *Radioactive Waste Management*, 3/2012, http://www.world-nuclear.org/info/Nuclear-Fuel-Cycle/Nuclear-Wastes/Radioactive-Waste-Management/#.UjNxUcaTiSo

[309] Wikipedia, *Thorium*, http://en.wikipedia.org/wiki/Thorium

[310] Ibid

[311] World Nuclear Association, *Thorium*, 6/2013, http://www.world-nuclear.org/info/Current-and-Future-Generation/Thorium/#.Uidv9pKTiSo

312 Ibid

313 Extreme Tech, *Thorium nuclear reactor trial begins, could provide cleaner, safer, almost-waste-free energy*, Sebastian Anthony, 7/1/2013, http://www.extremetech.com/extreme/160131-thorium-nuclear-reactor-trial-begins-could-provide-cleaner-safer-almost-waste-free-energy

314 Ibid

315 Howstuffworks, *Are oil companies promoting alternative energy?*, Alison Kim Perry, http://auto.howstuffworks.com/fuel-efficiency/biofuels/oil-companies-promoting-alternative-energy.htm

316 Boundless.com, Introduction, *Every product goes through the various life cycle phases of introduction, growth, maturity and decline*, https://www.boundless.com/marketing/products/product-life-cycles/introduction/

317 Goodreads.com, http://www.goodreads.com/quotes/446497-we-do-not-inherit-the-earth-from-our-ancestors-we

318 Wikipedia, *List of scientists opposing the mainstream scientific assessment of global warming*, http://en.wikipedia.org/wiki/List_of_scientists_opposing_the_mainstream_scientific_assessment_of_global_warming

319 Forbes, *Global Warming Alarmists Caught Doctoring '97-Percent Consensus Claims*, James Taylor, 5/30/2013, http://www.forbes.com/sites/jamestaylor/2013/05/30/global-warming-alarmists-caught-doctoring-97-percent-consensus-claims/

320 Emsnews, *Sun Spots Vanish And Global Warming Is Freezing Cold: NOAA Finally Admits Sun Causes Weather*, 4/2/2013,

http://emsnews.wordpress.com/2013/04/02/sun-spots-vanish-and-global-warming-is-freezing-cold-noaa-finally-admits-sun-causes-weather/

321 Ecosystem-based Management Tools Network, *Climate Change Vulnerability Assessment and Adaptation Tools*, http://www.ebmtoolsdatabase.org/resource/climate-change-vulnerability-assessment-and-adaptation-tools

322 The Telegraph, *Global Warming? No, actually we're cooling, claim scientists*, Hayley Dixon, 9/8/2013, http://www.telegraph.co.uk/earth/environment/climatechange/10294082/Global-warming-No-actually-were-cooling-claim-scientists.html

323 Ibid

324 Ibid

325 World Coal Association, *Frequently Asked Questions*, http://www.worldcoal.org/resources/frequently-asked-questions/

326 The Global Warming Policy Foundation, *CHINA & INDIA ARE BUILDING 4 NEW COAL POWER PLANTS – EVERY WEEK*, Peter Galuszka, 11/14/2012, http://www.thegwpf.org/china-india-building-4-coal-power-plants-week/

327 The Raw Story, The Guardian, *U.S. and China agree to expand efforts to reduce greenhouse gas emissions*, Suzanne Goldenberg, 7/10/2013, http://www.rawstory.com/rs/2013/07/10/u-s-and-china-agree-to-expand-efforts-to-reduce-greenhouse-gas-emissions/

328 Brainyquote.com, http://www.brainyquote.com/quotes/quotes/r/richardarm107283.html

329 Neuromarketing, *Emotional Ads Work Best*, 7/27/2009, http://www.neurosciencemarketing.com/blog/article s/emotional-ads-work-best.htm

330 You Set the Pace, *Using Both Logic and Emotion to Fine Tune Your Decision Making Process*, Sean Davis, 1/2/2012, http://yousetthepace.com/logic-emotion/

331 NPR, *What Now? Obama Leads Polarized Government Into Second Term*, Alan Greenblatt, 1/21/2013, http://www.npr.org/blogs/itsallpolitics/2013/01/16/1 69520525/what-now-obama-leads-polarized-government-into-second-term
The Washington Post, *Obama: The most polarizing president. Ever.*, Chris Cillizza and Aaron Blake, 1/30/2012, http://www.washingtonpost.com/blogs/the-fix/post/obama-the-most-polarizing-president-ever/2012/01/29/gIQAmmkBbQ_blog.html

332 Voteview blog, Nolan McCarty, Keith T. Poole, Howard Rosenthal, *Polarization is Real (and Asymmetric)*, Christopher Hare, 5/15/2012, http://voteview.com/blog/?p=494

333 Silver City Sun-News, *The most transparent administration is unraveling*, 7/25/2013, http://www.scsun-news.com/ci_23721926

334 The Washington Post, *Run for cover: it's the most 'severe' liberal media bias in 25 years*, Jennifer Harper, 7/14/2013, http://www.washingtontimes.com/blog/watercooler/ 2013/jul/14/hold-tight-its-most-severe-liberal-media-bias-25-y/

Wikipedia, *Media bias in the United States*, http://en.wikipedia.org/wiki/Media_bias_in_the_U nited_States

[335] New Jersey News, *Term 'racist; too often used to silence dissenting views*, Ellen Dooley, 8/25/2009, http://www.nj.com/cranford/index.ssf/2009/08/ter m_racist_too_often_used_to.html

[336] Boston Herald.com, *MSNBC perfects playing the race card*, Jonah Goldberg, 8/26/2013, http://bostonherald.com/news_opinion/opinion/op_ ed/2013/08/msnbc_perfects_playing_the_race_card

Mediaite, *Race to the Bottom: Schultz Forgets Fellow Dems, Fellow MSNBC Hosts When Playing the Race Card on Syria*, Joe Concha, 9/6/2013, http://www.mediaite.com/tv/race-to-the-bottom-schultz-forgets-fellow-dems-fellow-msnbc-hosts-when-playing-the-race-card-on-syria/

[337] Journal Star, *Forum: Grow up, America, and stop playing the race card*, 8/30/2013, http://www.pjstar.com/opinions/forum/x128195343 4/Forum-Grow-up-America-and-stop-playing-the-race-card

[338] Accuracy in Media, *Rather Blasts Corporate-Owned Media, Praises Occupy Movement*, Don Irvine, 11/26/2011, http://www.aim.org/don-irvine-blog/rather-blasts-corporate-owned-media-praises-occupy-movement/

The Washington Free Beacon, *Carter praises 'successful' Occupy Movement*, 2/16/2012, http://freebeacon.com/carter-praises-successful-occupy-movement/

MRC Business and Media Institute, *$3.6 Million from Soros Aids Groups That Support, Promote Occupy Wall Street*, Iris Somberg, 10/13/2011, http://www.mrc.org/business-and-media-institute/36-million-soros-aids-groups-support-promote-occupy-wall-street

[339] Outside the Beltway, *Is It Racist To Oppose Barack Obama?*, James Joyner, 5/23/2012, http://www.outsidethebeltway.com/is-it-racist-to-oppose-barack-obama/

[340] The Washington Post, *America is neither left nor right but centrist*, Kathleen Parker, 3/21/2010, http://www.washingtonpost.com/wp-dyn/content/article/2010/03/19/AR2010031903702.html

[341] Smartbrief.com, http://www.smartbrief.com/quote/01/22/14/decent-and-manly-examination-acts-government-should-be-not-only-tolerated-encouraged#.Uu_rJBBdWa8

[342] Washington Post, *Federal government continues to lose billions to waste, fraud and abuse*, 3/10/2013, http://www.washingtonpost.com/business/capitalbusiness/federal-government-continues-to-lose-billions-to-waste-fraud-and-abuse/2013/03/08/a3fb7736-82b5-11e2-b99e-6baf4ebe42df_story.html

[343] U.S. House of Representatives Committee on Oversight and Government Reform, *Uncovering Waste, Fraud and Abuse in the Medicaid Program*, 4/25/2012, http://oversight.house.gov/wp-content/uploads/2012/04/Uncovering-Waste-Fraud-and-Abuse-in-the-Medicaid-Program-Final-3.pdf
Washington Post, *Federal government continues to lose billions to waste, fraud and abuse*, Angie Petty, 3/10/2013, http://www.washingtonpost.com/business/capitalbusiness/federal-government-continues-to-lose-billions-to-waste-fraud-and-abuse/2013/03/08/a3fb7736-82b5-11e2-b99e-6baf4ebe42df_story.html

[344] Council of the Inspectors General on Integrity and Efficiency, http://www.ignet.gov/

[345] HHS OIG Work Plan / FY 2013, *Part IV, Legal and Investigative Activities Related to Medicare and Medicaid*, http://oig.hhs.gov/reports-and-publications/archives/workplan/2013/WP04-CMS_Legal.pdf

[346] Ibid

[347] Office of Inspector General, *U.S. Department of Health & Human Services, Fugitive Profiles*, http://oig.hhs.gov/fraud/fugitives/profiles.asp#allonce

[348] Ibid

[349] Goodreads.com, http://www.goodreads.com/quotes/31589-the-government-is-merely-a-servant-merely-a-temporary-servant-it

[350] Salary.com, Bill Coleman, *Compensation Surveys*, http://www.salary.com/compensation-surveys/

[351] Government Executive, *No perfect way to compare private and public sector pay, study finds*, Amanda Palleschi, 7/24/2012, http://www.govexec.com/pay-benefits/2012/07/no-perfect-way-compare-private-and-public-sector-pay-study-finds/56975/

[352] Ibid

[353] CBO, *Comparing the Compensation of Federal and Private-Sector Employees*, 1/2012, http://www.cbo.gov/sites/default/files/cbofiles/attachments/01-30-FedPay.pdf

[354] Ibid

[355] Ibid

[356] National Journal, *Why It Is So Hard to Fire a Low-Performing Government Employee?*, Michael Catalini, 5/26/2013, http://www.nationaljournal.com/politics/why-is-it-

so-hard-to-fire-a-low-performing-government-employee-20130524

MSPB.org, *Federal Employee Termination Procedures*, http://www.mspb.org/Federal-employee-termination-procedures.html

USA Today, *Some federal workers more likely to die than lose jobs*, Dennis Cauchon, 7/19/2011, http://usatoday30.usatoday.com/news/washington/2011-07-18-fderal-job-security_n.htm

[357] Ibid

[358] Ibid

[359] Federal Times, *Federal pension systems' unfunded liabilities skyrocket*, Stephen Losey, 2/20/2013, http://www.federaltimes.com/article/20130220/BENEFITS02/302200001/Federal-pension-systems-8217-unfunded-liabilities-skyrocket

[360] Money News, *Unfunded Federal Pension Liabilities Head Skyward*, John Morgan, 2/22/2013, http://www.moneynews.com/FinanceNews/unfunded-pension-liability-govt/2013/02/22/id/491518

[361] FedSmith.com, *Federal Deficits and Your Federal Employee Retirement*, Ralph Smith, 2/21/2013, http://www.fedsmith.com/2013/02/21/federal-deficits-and-your-federal-employee-retirement/

USA Today, *Federal retirement plans almost as costly as Social Security*, Dennis Cauchon, 9/29/2011, http://usatoday30.usatoday.com/news/washington/story/2011-10-11/federal-retirement-pension-benefits/50592474/1

[362] Pensions & Investments, *Derailing pension reforms*, 9/2/2013, http://www.pionline.com/article/20130902/PRINTSUB/309029999

[363] National Conference of State Legislatures, *State Pension Reform, 2009-2011*, Ron Snell, 3/2012,

http://www.ncsl.org/issues-research/labor/state-pension-reform-2009-to-2011.aspx

364 Harvard Kennedy School Mossavar-Rahmani Center for Business and Government, *Underfunded Public Pensions in the United States: The Size of the Problem, the Obstacles to Reform and the Path Forward*, Thomas J. Healey, Carl Hess, Kevin Nicholson, 4/5/2012, http://www.hks.harvard.edu/var/ezp_site/storage/fckeditor/file/pdfs/centers-programs/centers/mrcbg/publications/fwp/MRCBG_FWP_2012_08-Healey_Underfunded.pdf

365 The New York Times, *A Generation Hobbled by the Soaring Cost of College*, Andrew Martin and Andrew W. Lehren, 5/12/2012, http://www.nytimes.com/2012/05/13/business/student-loans-weighing-down-a-generation-with-heavy-debt.html?pagewanted=all&_r=0

366 The Guardian, *The American dream should really be called the American debt*, Chris Williams, 8/27/2013, http://www.theguardian.com/commentisfree/2013/aug/27/student-loan-debt-cripple-young-americans

367 Ibid

368 CNBC, *Millennials' Ball and Chain: Student Loan Debt*, Hadley Malcolm, 7/1/2013, http://www.cnbc.com/id/100856310

369 Ibid

370 SFGate.com, *Feds take over student loan program from banks*, 3/30/2010, http://www.sfgate.com/business/networth/article/Feds-take-over-student-loan-program-from-banks-3193888.php

371 The Washington Post, *Obama signs student loan interest rate legislation into law*, Jenna Johnson,

9/9/2013, http://articles.washingtonpost.com/2013-08-09/politics/41223761_1_interest-rates-plus-loans-graduate-students

[372] USA TODAY, Detroit Free Press, *Government projects to make $50B in student loan profit*, David Jesse, 6/16/2013, http://www.usatoday.com/story/news/2013/06/16/us-government-projected-to-make-record-50b-in-student-loan-profit/2427443/

[373] The Huffington Post, *Student Loan Forgiveness Program Available To Millions Who Aren't Utilizing It, CFPB Says*, Philip Elliott, 8/28/2013, http://www.huffingtonpost.com/2013/08/28/student-loan-forgiveness-cfpb_n_3833832.html

[374] Forbes, *Thanks to Obamacare, A 20,000 Doctor Shortage Is Set To Quintuple*, Sally Pipes, 6/10/2013, http://www.forbes.com/sites/sallypipes/2013/06/10/thanks-to-obamacare-a-20000-doctor-shortage-is-set-to-quintuple/

[375] The Huffington Post, *Cost Of College Degree In U.S. Has Increased 1,120 Percent In 30 Years, Report Says*, 8/15/2012, http://www.huffingtonpost.com/2012/08/15/cost-of-college-degree-increase-12-fold-1120-percent-bloomberg_n_1783700.html

[376] Business Insider, *Health Care Costs Are Still Rising Faster Than Workers Can Keep Up*, Mandi Woodruff, 8/22/2013, http://www.businessinsider.com/health-care-costs-are-still-rising-faster-than-workers-can-keep-up-2013-8

JP's, *Real Estate Charts*, http://www.jparsons.net/housingbubble/

[377] NAICU, *Cost Cutting and Efficiency Initiatives at Private Colleges and Universities*,

http://www.naicu.edu/special_initiatives/affordabilit
y/news_room/

378 Creditcards.com, *What the credit card reform law means to you*, Connie Parker,
http://www.creditcards.com/credit-card-news/help/what-the-new-credit-card-rules-mean-6000.php

379 NOLO, *What Happens If You Default on Your Student Loans*, http://www.nolo.com/legal-encyclopedia/default-student-loan-29859.html

380 Eagleform.org,
http://www.eagleforum.org/educate/washington/advice.html

381 Bloomberg Businessweek, *A Smaller, Cheaper, Stronger Military*, Paul M. Barrett, 11/8/2012,
http://www.businessweek.com/articles/2012-11-08/a-smaller-cheaper-stronger-military

382 Whitehouse.gov, Office of Science and Technology Policy, *OSTP Initiatives*,
http://www.whitehouse.gov/administration/eop/ostp/initiatives

383 Forio.com, *U.S. STEM Education Model*,
http://forio.com/simulate/bhef/u-s-stem-education-model/overview/

384 CNN.com, *CNN Explains: U.S. drones*,
http://www.cnn.com/2013/02/07/politics/drones-cnn-explains/

385 Brainyquote.com,
http://www.brainyquote.com/quotes/quotes/b/benjaminca490177.html

386 NBC News, *Obamacare glitches: Gov't contract for troubled site has swelled; GOP targest Sebelius*, Tom Costello and Erin McClam, 10/18/2013,
http://usnews.nbcnews.com/_news/2013/10/18/210

25507-obamacare-glitches-govt-contract-for-troubled-site-has-swelled-gop-targets-sebelius?lite

[387] Ibid

[388] NBCNews.com, *Hackers: HealthCare.gov still riddled with potential security issues*, Julianne Pepitone, 1/16/2014, http://www.nbcnews.com/technology/hackers-healthcare-gov-still-riddled-potential-security-issues-2D11940198

[389] The Washington Post, *Obamacare needs young people to sign up. And it looks like they're starting.*, Sarah Kliff, 10/11/2013, http://www.washingtonpost.com/blogs/wonkblog/wp/2013/10/11/obamacare-needs-young-people-to-sign-up-and-it-looks-like-theyre-starting/

[390] Ibid

[391] Forbes, *Interactive Map: In 13 States Plus D.C., Obamacare Will Increase Health Premiums By 24% On Average*, Avik Roy, 9/4/2013, http://www.forbes.com/sites/theapothecary/2013/09/04/interactive-map-in-13-states-plus-d-c-individual-health-premiums-will-increase-by-an-average-of-24/

[392] Ibid

[393] HHS.gov, *Key Features of the Affordable Care Act By Year*, http://www.hhs.gov/healthcare/facts/timeline/timeline-text.html

[394] Association of American Medical Colleges, *Projected Supply and Demand, Physicians, 2008-2020*, https://www.aamc.org/advocacy/campaigns_and_coalitions/fixdocshortage/

[395] Ibid

[396] Wnd.com, *Obamacare Has Doctors Planning Exit*, Bob Unruh, 7/19/2013,

http://www.wnd.com/2013/07/obamacare-has-doctors-planning-exit/

397 Forbes.com, *The Fourth Obamacare Shock Wave Is About To Reach Us*, Jim Powell, 11/13/2013, http://www.forbes.com/sites/jimpowell/2013/11/13/the-fourth-obamacare-shock-wave-is-about-to-reach-us/

398 AMA Association.org, Practicing Medicine, *Four key steps to begin practicing medicine in the U.S.*, http://www.ama-assn.org//ama/pub/about-ama/our-people/member-groups-sections/international-medical-graduates/practicing-medicine.page

Remapping Debate.org, *Recruitment of foreign physicians: a zero-sum equation?*, Mike Alberti, 3/9/2011, http://www.remappingdebate.org/article/recruitment-foreign-physicians-zero-sum-equation

399 Doctors Recruitment.com, *Doctors Recruitment Australia,* http://doctorsrecruitment.com/ Halth.gov.sk.ca, *Physician Recruitment Strategy*, http://www.health.gov.sk.ca/adx/aspx/adxGetMedia.aspx?DocID=1633ff92-37fa-4ece-b798-1b8144d21420

400 Washington Examiner.com, *CBO: Obamacare costs double to $1.8 trillion in first decade*, Philip Klein, 5/14/2013, http://washingtonexaminer.com/cbo-obamacare-costs-double-to-1.8-trillion-in-first-decade/article/2529655

401 Ibid

402 First Read on NBC News.com, *Poll: Majority think health law needs overhaul or elimination*, Domenico Montanaro, 10/30/2013, http://firstread.nbcnews.com/_news/2013/10/30/21

252291-poll-majority-think-health-law-needs-overhaul-or-elimination?lite

403 CNSnews.com, *Waxman on 10,535 Pages of Obamacare Regs: 'Is It Important That I Read It?'*, Penny Starr, 10/2/2013, http://www.cnsnews.com/news/article/penny-starr/waxman-10535-pages-obamacare-regs-it-important-i-read-it

404 Washington Post.com, *How many pages of regulations for 'Obamacare'?*, Glenn Kessler, 5/15/2013, http://www.washingtonpost.com/blogs/fact-checker/post/how-many-pages-of-regulations-for-obamacare/2013/05/14/61eec914-bcf9-11e2-9b09-1638acc3942e_blog.html

405 Newsbuster.org, *Maher: Sure Obama Lied But He Had to or Obamacare Might Not Have Passed*, Noel Sheppard, 10/29/2013, http://newsbusters.org/blogs/noel-sheppard/2013/10/29/maher-obama-had-lie-about-people-keeping-health-plans-or-obamacare-mi
First Read on NBC News.com, *Poll: Majority think health law needs overhaul or elimination*, Domenico Montanaro, 10/30/2013, http://firstread.nbcnews.com/_news/2013/10/30/21 252291-poll-majority-think-health-law-needs-overhaul-or-elimination?lite

406 Huffington Post.com, *Union Support Waning for the Affordable Care Act: Look for the Union Label on Obamacare? Perhaps Not*, Wendy N. Powell, 6/13/2013, http://www.huffingtonpost.com/wendy-n-powell/union-support-waning-for-b_3435163.html

[407] The New Media Journal.us, *Obamacare Mandate 30-Hour Week As 'Full-Time' Employment*, http://newmediajournal.us/indx.php/item/7243
[408] AMA.com, American Medical Association, *Independent Payment Advisory Board*, http://www.ama-assn.org/ama/pub/advocacy/topics/independent-payment-advisory-board.page?
[409] The Atlantic.com, *27% of Surgeons Still Think Obamacare Has Death Panels*, Olga Khazan, 12/19/2013, http://www.theatlantic.com/health/archive/2013/12/27-of-surgeons-still-think-obamacare-has-death-panels/282534/
[410] Nationalreview.com, National Review Online, *Twenty-Seven Obamacare Changes*, Grace-Marie Turner & Tyler Hartsfield, 11/15/2013, http://www.nationalreview.com/article/364080/twenty-seven-obamacare-changes-grace-marie-turner-tyler-hartsfield
[411] Ibid
[412] Galen.org, Galen Institute, *The IRS and its 46 new powers to enforce Obamacare*, 6/5/2013, http://www.galen.org/2013/46-new-irs-powers-to-enforce-obamacare/
[413] FactCheck.org, *IRS and the Health Care Law, Part II*, 2/18/2011 and updated 2/23/2011, http://www.factcheck.org/2011/02/irs-and-the-health-care-law-part-ii/
[414] IRS.gov, *Do I have to File a Tax Return?*, 1/4/2011, http://www.irs.gov/uac/Do-I-have-to-File-a-Tax-Return%3F
[415] IRS.gov, *Affordable Care Act Tax Provisions*, http://www.irs.gov/uac/Affordable-Care-Act-Tax-Provisions

[416] International Business Times, *Under Obama Health Care Law: Government-Controlled Private Insurance*, Besty McCaughey, 2/27/2013, http://www.ibtimes.com/under-obama-health-care-law-government-controlled-private-insurance-1106097

[417] Las Vegas Sun.com, *Reid says Obamacare just a step toward eventual single-payer system*, Karoun Demirjian, 8/10/2013, http://www.lasvegassun.com/news/2013/aug/10/reid-says-obamacare-just-step-toward-eventual-sing/

[418] Ibid

[419] Forbes.com, Dear Speaker Pelosi, *We've Looked Inside Obamacare And It's Really Bad*, John Cohrssen & John Hoff, 11/11/2013, http://www.forbes.com/sites/realspin/2013/11/11/dear-speaker-pelosi-weve-looked-inside-obamacare-and-its-really-bad/

[420] Goodreads.com, http://www.goodreads.com/quotes/63485-common-sense-is-the-most-widely-shared-commodity-in-the

[421] FT.com, *Learn from the fall of Rome, US warned*, Jeremy Grant, 9/14/2007, http://www.ft.com/intl/cms/s/0/80fa0a2c-49ef-11dc-9ffe-0000779fd2ac.html#axzz2qW4XWkq6
Salon.com, *8 striking parallels between the U.S. and the Roman Empire*, Steven Strauss, 12/26/2012, http://www.salon.com/2012/12/26/8_striking_parallels_between_the_u_s_and_the_roman_empire/
Forbes.com, *The Decline And Fall Of The American Empire?*, Keith Roberts, 5/25/2011, http://www.forbes.com/2011/05/25/decline-and-fall-of-the-american-empire.html

[422] Ibid

[423] Washington Post.com, *Audit details lavish spending at IRS conference*, Lisa Rein, 6/4/2013, http://www.washingtonpost.com/politics/audit-details-lavish-spending-at-irs-conference/2013/06/04/3245721c-cd52-11e2-8f6b-67f40e176f03_story.html
NY Dailynews.com, *IRS official apologizes for wasting funds on 'Star Trek' spoof video*, Dan Friedman, 6/6/2013, http://www.nydailynews.com/news/national/irs-official-apologizes-star-trek-spoof-video-article-1.1365589
CNBC.com, *IRS Officials Face Grilling Over Lavish Spending*, 6/6/2013, http://www.cnbc.com/id/100794596
Washington Post.com, *Everything you need to know about the IRS scandal in one FAQ*, Dylan Matthews, 5/14/2013, http://www.washingtonpost.com/blogs/wonkblog/wp/2013/05/14/everything-you-need-to-know-about-the-irs-scandal-in-one-faq/
[424] NYTimes.com, *Phone Records of Journalists Seized by U.S.*, Charlie Savage and Leslie Kaufman, 5/13/2013, http://www.nytimes.com/2013/05/14/us/phone-records-of-journalists-of-the-associated-press-seized-by-us.html?_r=0
Huffington Post.com, *Fox News Erupts Over James Rosen Scandal, Says His Parents' Records Were Seized (VIDEO)*, Jack Mirkinson, 5/22/2013, http://www.huffingtonpost.com/2013/05/22/fox-news-james-rosen-parents-white-house-doj_n_3318733.html
Daily News.com, *Benghazi attack: New report shows the real scandal isn't what Obama called it*, Ryan

Beckwith, 1/15/2014,
http://www.dailynews.com/general-news/20140115/benghazi-attack-new-report-shows-the-real-scandal-isnt-what-obama-called-it

[425] Forbes.com, *The Federal Reserve's Explicit Goal: Devalue The Dollar 33%*, Charles Kadlec, 2/6/2012, http://www.forbes.com/sites/charleskadlec/2012/02/06/the-federal-reserves-explicit-goal-devalue-the-dollar-33/

CBS NEWS.com, *National Debt has increased more under Obama than under Bush*, Mark Knoller, 3/19/2012, http://www.cbsnews.com/news/national-debt-has-increased-more-under-obama-than-under-bush/

Investors.com, Investor's Business Daily, *Dependency Index Surges 23% Under President Obama*, John Merline, 2/8/2012, http://news.investors.com/business/020812-600452-government-dependence-jumps-under-president-obama.htm

[426] Gallup.com, *Americans See More Economic Harm Than Good in Health Law*, Frank Newport, 7/5/2012, http://www.gallup.com/poll/155513/americans-economic-harm-good-health-law.aspx

[427] Goodreads.com, Thomas Paine>Quotes>*Quotable Quote*, http://www.goodreads.com/quotes/129333-i-love-the-man-that-can-smile-in-trouble-that